Unfinish
Journe

To Coleen

with Best wishes

[signature]

First published in Britain in 2006 by *The Polemicist* in conjunction
with Artery Publications, II Dorset Road, London W5 4HU

Photographs are from the Morris family archives apart from the photos of Cable Street Battle commemorative plaque on
page 53 which is reproduced courtesy of LB Tower Hamlets; Cable Street mural on page 55 courtesy of Desmond Rochfort
and Tottenham Hotspur photograph on page 140 by Action Images Ltd.

Designed by Michal Boñcza of Artloud (www.artloud.com)

Printed by Lithosphere
ACIP catalogue record for this book is available from the British Library
ISBN 0-9513909-8-8
ISBN 13 978-0-9513909-8-6

Unfinished Journey

Aubrey Morris

"What kind of peace do I mean? What kind of peace do we seek? Not a Pax Americana enforced on the world by American weapons of war. Not the peace of the grave or the security of the slave. I am talking about genuine peace, the kind of peace that makes life on earth worth living, the kind that enables men and nations to grow and to hope and to build a better life for their children − not merely peace for Americans but peace for all men and women − not merely peace in our time but peace for all time."

President John F. Kennedy
10 June 1963

I dream a world where man
No other man will scorn,
Where love will bless the earth
And peace its path adorn
I dream a world where all
Will know sweet freedom's way.
Where greed no longer saps the soul
Nor avarice blights our day.
A world I dream where black or white,
Whatever race you be,
Will share the bounties of the earth
And every man is free,
Where wretchedness will hang its head
And joy, like a pearl, attends the needs of all mankind −
Of such I dream, my world.

Langston Hughes

Unfinished Journey is more than anything a continuing quest, for realistic and radical solutions to injustice. Aubrey's passionate principles, his curiosity, his enthusiasm and
his conscientiousness take him from the battle of Cable Street through the competitive struggles of the tourist industry to the tempestuous conviviality of the Anjou Luncheon Club, collecting colourful friends along the way and becoming ever more determined in his search for a feasible socialism. Angry now at the 'catastrophe of New Labour', but confident that, somehow, there can be alternatives, he inspires all of us who follow his quest. Rarely has such a story been told and even more rarely has it been told so well.
It's truly 'bull's bood' to revive an anaemic political culture.

Hilary Wainwright
Editor *Red Pepper*

From knowledge to knowledge: Aubrey, having undertaken 'the knowledge' of a London cabbie – and duly qualified, became fully street wise and entrepreneurial – talents which he was able to apply to his next venture: the package holiday business.

As one of the early pioneers in the embryo stages of package development – and at a dynamic time when many were trying to establish themselves in the travel trade – Aubrey shone immediately, in no small way due to his charismatic, open personality. He soon became a 'friend to all'.

As a result of Aubrey's expertise and success, Riviera became the perfect acquisition for the Thomson Holiday Group – of which Aubrey became Managing Director.
The package holiday business is highly indebted to the vision and hard work of Aubrey Morris.

Guilio Ugo
Former President of the Chartered Institute of Travel Marketing

The anecdotes about the characters who inhabited the travel industry in the 20th century provide a fascinating insight into the entrepreneurs who created what is now the world's biggest industry. He was a pioneer in the air charter holiday business and provides an insight into the events of that time. He knew most if not all of the people in the business intimately and contributed hugely to the time and the place and the being.

Aubrey was and still is a convinced Communist. He was and still is a successful capitalist! This massive contradiction disturbed him greatly when the expansion of Riviera Holidays necessitated dealing with Franco's fascist Spain. How did he deal with this dilemma? Behind every great man there is an amazing woman - in this case, Lily. The distribution channels for holidays may have changed but the fundamental economics are still the same as when tour operating began. Sell more holidays after breakeven point has been reached and profits will be made.

Allan Beaver
Professor Allan Beaver is the vice president of the Chartered Institute on Marketing Travel Group and the author of many books on the travel industry, including *A Dictionary of Travel and Tourism*

CONTENTS

FOREWORD

As a journalist on the *Guardian*, I receive lots of invitations to speak. Some are rejected, some are accepted with reluctance, some with enthusiasm at the time of asking but with a sense of foreboding as the day in question nears. But there is one summons to speak that I always look forward to: the invitation to the gathering of the Anjou Luncheon Club on the first Thursday of every month upstairs at the Gay Hussar in Soho's Greek Street. I use the word summons deliberately, because in their time just about every commentator on the Guardian has been called upon to outline their political ideas over the cherry soup and the roast duck with Hungarian potatoes. The lunch starts at 12.30 prompt and woe betide the guest who turns up late, cancels or, even worse, comes unprepared for what is a rigorous examination.

If that makes it sound as if the lunch is an austere occasion, nothing could be further from the truth. True, this is an occasion for left-wing politics (of the old rather than the new variety) and the level of debate is high. But is also the most glorious fun. As a guest, you are expected to speak for around 20 minutes and then let the members have their say. And have their say they certainly do. If he or she chooses, the guest can happily slurp their way through a couple of bottles of Bulls Blood oblivious to the argument raging around them. But few resist the temptation to have their four penn'orth. I'm sure the members of the Anjou Luncheon Club will not mind me saying so, but few of them are in the first flush of youth, but they make up for it with their passion for radical politics.

So that's how I came to know Aubrey Morris. I had the summons from Aubrey a decade or more back, and I've been going back once a year on the first Thursday of the month ever since to talk about globalisation, Africa, Europe, the environment, Labour's record in power, anything so long as it gets the intellectual juices going. At one gathering, I was told that next month's speaker was to be Ed Balls, then chief economist at the Treasury and Gordon Brown's right-hand man. A couple of weeks later he phoned demanding: "What have you been saying to the Anjou Luncheon Club? They're really fired up and you're to blame".

Actually, I wasn't to blame. It didn't take me to fire up this collection of renegade socialists, Marxists and radicals of various hues from London's Jewish Diaspora. They were fired up enough already, and as you read Aubrey's memoirs you can see why. A product of an East End upbringing, his socialism was forged in the poverty and the anti-fascist struggles of that era. The account of the fight against Mosley's blackshirts is especially vivid.

In later life, Aubrey went on to become a successful businessman. Little did I know as a seven-year-old allowed to stay up to watch my beloved Tottenham Hotspur become the first British club to win a European trophy in May 1963 that it had been Aubrey's pioneering charter company that had airlifted 2000 Spurs fans to Rotterdam to watch the mighty lilywhites thrash Athletico Madrid 5-1. My personal contact with Aubrey came much later, but these memoirs help fill in some of the gaps in my knowledge of his rich and varied life. I shall go on looking forward to my annual summons from the Anjou Luncheon Club for as long as my good friend Aubrey sees fit to invite me. I hope that will be for many years to come.

Larry Elliott

INTRODUCTION

As I write I realise that I've been involved in grass roots politics, in one way or another, for over seven decades. During that time, I belonged to two political parties, but for most of it I was a member of none. My working life, for almost half a century was spent in the travel and tourist business, from the very beginnings of mass tourism. This autobiographical memoir charts my political development and my central involvement in the rise and expansion of mass tourism − something taken for granted today, but when I was a youngster even to travel across the Channel was beyond most working people's wildest dreams.

My political life is symptomatic of many of my generation and background − sons and daughters of Jewish immigrants who settled in London's East End during the nineteenth and early twentieth centuries. My contemporaries were people like Alfie Bass, Harry Gold, Lionel Bart, Solly Kaye, Phil Piratin, Stanley Forman and dozens of like-minded youngsters who came into left wing politics as a result of their family background, the demands of the times and a yearning for justice and an end to poverty.

Our families' lives were steeped in East European and Jewish culture; our immediate ancestors had been victims of pogroms and persecution and suffered political exclusion. Fleeing the ghettos for a new life in a capitalist democracy, while offering relief on one level, was no bed of roses. Most of our families, at least in the early years after arrival, led lives of dire poverty, still experienced anti-Semitism, even if not of the vicious East European variety, and struggled to survive in a country, which was hardly welcoming.

Those of my generation, growing up in the nineteen twenties and thirties, suffered the after-effects of the First World War, the poverty and unemployment, and then the seemingly inevitable rise of fascism. But we youngsters had begun to think and behave differently from our parents. We weren't going to take the threat of new pogroms and persecution lying down. Our experiences and our history led many of us to dedicate our lives to an ideal, a vision born out of the travails of the period.

The twists and turns of the political process during those decades and the eventual cataclysmic events unleashed by German fascism forced us to continually evolve new ideas. Sometimes we saw small developments as victories, but many of these proved, in the end, to be unsustainable or mere mirages.

In the last decades of the twentieth century and into the twenty first, the Anjou Luncheon Club has been central to my continuing political engagement from a Left perspective and has proved to be a way of engaging with a new political generation, engendering new ideas and firing a new enthusiasm. The Anjou Luncheon Club was set up by me and a small group of like-minded individuals, from a similar background and of the same generation, in order to help us keep alive an intellectual ferment during a period when politics seemed to degenerate into mere party politicking and spin. (See chapter 25 for a more detailed description of the Club's genesis and the role it has played over recent years)

My life-long involvement in the travel industry came about serendipitously and was not a conscious career decision on my part. Nevertheless in a very short period of time I found myself as one of the early pioneers and initiators of the package holiday phenomenon. I progressed, in less than five years, from being an ordinary driver of a London black cab to become chief executive of Europe's largest air tour operator. But my strong left-wing views were little compromised, despite the transformation in my economic status. In my business role, I met and had dealings with many of the captains of industry at that time, and this was something that tended to reinforce my political beliefs, rather than undermine them.

To be involved in the travel business in those early days was both fascinating and exhilarating. It was uncharted territory, without limits and open to anyone with ideas, vision and dedication. Of course, like so many revolutionary developments, it was dependent on the work that had been done before and, above all, by the simultaneous emergence of advanced technology, particularly passenger aeroplanes. It was also made possible by the advances made in the post-war class struggle, which had won for working people an income allowing them to do more than simply feed and clothe their families. For the first time in history we had a generation with a disposable income for leisure activities and with more time to enjoy that leisure.

That is a bullet-point summary of my lfe. In the following pages I provide embellishment and, hopefully, flesh it out with more personal detail and historical context.

Why have I decided to write my life story? I suppose the easy answer is that, over the years, when I have talked of my experiences, people have often said to me, 'you should write a book', but in doing so there is of course also something of an ego trip involved. I've also always had a desire to write something, but never felt I had the ability. I'd already started writing a mystery story and managed two chapters, but lacked the confidence to complete it. Maybe if there is still time I'll pick it up again. Writing these autobiographical memoirs has been a challenge, but I managed it. I can only hope it will give readers some new insights, perhaps also pleasure and cause for thought.

CHAPTER ONE
Settling in to a new life

According to my late aunt Stella I am a direct descendant of a famous and heroic officer who served in the Tsarist Russian Army – a Field Marshall no less! To my aunt Raie, whose aspirations to grandeur were more modest, he was merely a Major General. My family were the descendants of Polish Jews who emigrated to London from Lodz during the outgoing decades of the 19th century to escape the persecution and the pogroms, yet they still gloried in their apocryphal lineage.

My uncle Woolfie, the youngest of that generation, gave me another version, but this too I found difficult to accept. Grandfather, he told me, had been pressganged into the Tsarist army at the age of twelve. A likely story, I thought to myself, but was intrigued sufficiently to eventually discover that it had really happened as he said.

The first partition of Poland by Russia in 1772 brought unwelcome guests into the Tsarist Empire – a vast influx of Jews. To the traditionally anti-Semitic Tsars this was the 'unfortunate' deficit on the balance sheet of territorial expansion. The Empress Elizabeth had personally issued a diktat for the expulsion of Jews in 1742. According to the legal record, there were, as a result of this diktat, comparatively few survivors by 1772. These new Jews from Poland were to face their worst period of persecution in the annals of Jewish martyrdom until the horrendous genocide of the Nazi Holocaust.

With the accession to the throne of Nicholas I (1825-55) there followed a systematic programme of Jewish extermination on Russian territory. Nicholas issued numerous decrees to this end, including selective conscription for Jewish boys between the ages of twelve and twenty-five, who were made to serve in the Russian army for up to thirty-one years. My great grandfather was one of those conscripts, but managed to survive all those marathon marches to far-flung corners of that vast Russian empire. His name was Aaron Itzach Putajevski. Eventually he married and had five children, one of whom, Eliyah Moishe, was my own grandfather. It was he who, with my grandmother Esther, made the arduous cross-country journey to London with their six children in 1902. My grandfather, like so many Jews, had an East European name that was, at least for the British, a tongue-twister. He soon dropped his surname Putajevski, and adopted the more prosaic one of Morris, becoming Alex Morris. Mind you, I am pleased that he took a name with such associations with the more renowned William Morris. Like William Morris, he was a craftsman too, a continental baker and pastry cook. In Lodz, on the border between Poland and Russia, he had owned and worked in a small bakery.

On arrival at London's East End docks, the best the family of seven could find were two cramped rooms above a fish and chip shop already tenanted by his brother-in-law, Isaac Levy, at 82 Cable Street. In a very short time, though, he was able to find a very small bakery with living accommodation in St. Georges Street, now known as the Highway. This he ran until he was offered a bigger one at 86 Cable Street, owned by a German, who several years earlier had come to England as a political refugee. The German owner had become perturbed by growing hostility towards all foreigners in Britain at the turn of the century, and decided to return home.

Alex Morris bought the business from him in 1904 for £5 in easy instalments! These new premises brought distinct advantages for the family. Above the shop there were several rooms, and in the rear there were two extraordinarily spacious rooms, one of which became the family living room. Equally important, this new space enabled my grandfather to teach his sons how to practise the trade and, vital in those days for family survival, to do it on low profit margins – it obviated the need to employ outsiders.

Cable Street is a long one, and only a short stretch, in which No. 86 was situated, could be considered Jewish in those days. Although there were numerous Jewish-owned shops and tailoring workshops in the vicinity and there were also cafes run by owners of various nationalities. On one side of the bakery was a boarding house for African seamen, and Mr. Royal who ran the premises was himself from West Africa and a highly respected member of the community. On the other side was a second-hand clothes shop run by a Mr. Yapp, a deeply religious Jew noted for his praying, to which he felt a particular compunction while travelling on the local trams, and when asked to pay his fare! Adjoining his prem-

Eliyah Moishe Putajevski, my grandfather, and family before emigration, Poland 1889.

ises, on the corner of North East Passage, was a fish shop belonging to Isaac Levy. Isaac was a giant of a man married to my grandmother's sister, and they had a half-brother, Beinish, who lived nearby.

Isaac rose regularly at 5am, walked to nearby Pell Street, at the junction with Cable Street, where he stabled his horse and cart. It was probably the narrowest part of what was already a very narrow street and, to make matters worse, there were bollards along its length. The early morning complex manoeuvring of his cart and horse, shouting instructions to the latter, always in Yiddish, was the alarm clock for many of the street's inhabitants to get out of bed.

My great aunt Kate's role in the fish and chip business, which she carried out most assiduously, as well as doing the household chores and raising their only child, Walter, was to pickle the onions and cucumbers that were a vital accompaniment along with the obligatory salt and vinegar. I recall her working in the

Eliyah Moishe Putajevski, now 'the English gentleman' Alex Morris, and family in 1908.

back room, surrounded by a mountain of string-sacks containing the scallions and small cucumbers. She would sit for hours peeling the onions without a tear in her eyes — I imagine the years of doing the job had made her immune to their pungency — and popping them into the large pickling jars. Also employed by my great uncle Isaac was his brother Munnas who lived in rooms above the shop with his wife Fageh and their three children.

Munnas was recognised as a 'character', whereas Isaac, although a giant of a man, was quiet, gentle and unobtrusive. Munnas was diminutive, erratic and fierce in manner and voice. In the late evening, on most days, there would be a long queue of customers waiting to be served. Fish and chips in those days were still cheap staples on working class dinner tables. Frequently anti-Semitic comments could be heard from the impatient queuers, and although Isaac would ignore them, Munnas would not. He would rush around the counter brandishing a sharp fish filleting knife or a shovel laden with hot coals and chase the malcontents from the shop. If he were sufficiently fired up he would chase the unfortunates far along Cable Street, and although he never caught them, you could be sure they wouldn't return to the shop in a hurry.

Cable Street was not very wide and still cobbled at that time; the pavements were narrow and the multi-storied premises on both sides cast constant shade over the road. Occasionally I would trek towards Leman Street until I reached

Feigenbaums, just past Back Church Lane, which had connotations of mysterious and illicit sex and thus held a strong fascination for young lads of my age. Local girls went there, I was told, for part-time prostitution. They were 'on the game'. It was seen, at least by some, as an easy way of obtaining extra cash in a period when jobs, even badly paid ones, particularly for women, were at a premium. Feigenbaums was a large open shop, stacked high with boxes of imported eggs, mostly from Poland. I was fascinated by the men 'kandling' (checking) the eggs for two things: one, to see whether they were too addled to eat, in which case they would be discarded and, two, if there were blood spots, they could not be sold to Jews on religious grounds. They examined the eggs through a hole in a cylindrical cover over a bright electric light.

Directly opposite our shop was a large, faceless factory building from which emanated a constant and tantalising aroma of roasting coffee. A hoist attached to the outer wall was used to lift the sacks of coffee beans delivered from the nearby docks. Most of the work in the factory, including lifting the heavy sacks, was done by women wearing long skirts covered with hessian sacking from old beanbags, and wearing flat caps. Many of these women behaved like men. They were real female proletarians and could give any man a run for his money in terms of rough language and bawdiness. On Friday nights they congregated in and around Gimmick's pub on the corner of Pell Street, downing pints, sometimes brawling, often raucous and frequently urinating openly in the street.

Pell Street was not much more than a wide alleyway lined by small terraced houses on either side and only patrolled by a local constable if accompanied by a fellow officer. The occupants of Pell Street were mainly Irish immigrant families, who worked as casual labourers in the docks. The Irish were dominant in the local community at the time and were mainly concentrated in Wapping, hence its nickname of County Wapping. The short stretch of Cable Street that I knew was quite incongruous in its ethnic mix – mainly Jewish within an enclave of ultra-Catholic Irish.

At the rear of Cable Street, and reached by North East Passage with Nathan Zlotnicki's tailoring emporium on the opposite corner, was Wellclose Square which was orignally built in 1728. This square could also be accessed from The Highway (then called St. Georges Street) through Grace's Alley and Ship Alley. One of the buildings here, on the corner of Ship Alley, was the Courthouse and Jail, where miscreants of all types were tried and, if guilty, incarcerated before transportation to Australia.

In Grace's Alley was the once famous Wilton's Music Hall, by then no longer used as such and already somewhat decrepit, and used for storage purposes. Today, of course, it has been restored to its earlier splendour. Wellclose Square was enclosed by dense terraces of Victorian houses clustered around a Catholic church and school. My uncle Woolfie remembers vividly that this particular square was taboo for him and his friends. The church and school were the centres of Catholicism in the district. It is from this patch that a generation of Stepney's Labour leaders emerged who, in the aftermath of the Second World War, took control of Stepney council for Labour after decades of Liberal and Conservative and Liberal domination. They ruled with Tammany like control, but unfortunately were as reactionary as anything before them. As in other urban areas of Britain, which came under the sway of Irish-Catholic Labourism, a cosy nepotism prevailed. This contrasted with the views and behaviour of Rev. Grozer, an eminent Church of England minister, who vigorously opposed bigotry and poverty in the area and, was the most liberal of men.

After the Second World War there was a widespread and urgent desire for a new and different kind of Britain — one of peace and plenty. For many there was also the desire for a socialist society, and the surprising Labour election victory of 1945 was an expression of that. In view of the role played by the Soviet Red Army and Communist-led resistance movements in the defeat of fascism, there was also an upsurge in votes for Communist candidates. In Stepney, Phil Piratin was elected as a Communist member of parliament and several Communist councillors were also elected, largely on the left wing Jewish vote — people like Max Levitas, Solly Kaye and Arnold Posner.

CHAPTER TWO
Growing up in London's East End

My father married Dora Sidlin who had arrived in London as a baby from Dvinsk in Latvia, together with two elder brothers and a sister. We occupied two rooms at 60 Princes Square, which was built at the same time as Wellclose Square, and was also used to house the Scandinavian community in Britain. We were just a few doors away from Dave Carson's Dairy that then housed a herd of cows, each of which had its own name. Most of the women had a particular favourite. My Bubba's was Gwyneth and despite her difficulty in pronouncing the Welsh name, she demanded that her milk came only from her. I often wondered, later, quite what my Bubba would have thought, to see me using the 'iron cow', a machine for dispensing milk into jugs or containers, which was open day and night and was operated by a small dairyman in The Oval, off Hackney Road.

I was born on 20th May 1919, only a year after the carnage of the First World War came to an end. By this time, both my parents were fluent in English since they had come over as small children; my mother a mere babe-in-arms. They did, though, speak Yiddish to each other if they wanted to hide something from us, thinking we wouldn't understand. At my grandparents Yiddish was the lingua franca too, but they also sometimes spoke English. I could understand their Yiddish, but of course didn't let on. I couldn't really speak it though – I think that was normal for my generation.

I started school at the early age of four, like all other children in Britain. I remember the afternoon sleeping period when the tables would be turned upside down and a hammock made using a sheet with metal rings attached at each corner connected to the four table legs, and in which we were supposed to sleep. Otherwise I recall little of my days at Christian Street Primary School, which I attended, and where Mr Solomon was the head. I do, though, recall my mother bringing me mugs of milky hot chocolate at break times which she, along with several other mothers, would slide under the gap at the bottom of the gate for us.

My father worked for his father, and one of my very first memories was of being lifted on to the workbench where my grandfather, together with my father and three of my uncles would be plaiting 'chollas'. This would be on Friday mornings and the bread would be sold for the Sabbath. Even then I admired their dexterity, speed of working, and the standard uniformity of the product. I later picked up their skills by watching and practising. The weighed dough would be torn into five almost equal pieces, each piece rolled into a strand tapered at both ends, placed symmetrically, then joined at one end and plaited into shape. Years later I could still make them.

An equally vivid memory, but very disturbing, was being wakened in the early hours of Saturday morning by my mother's strident voice. She would be berating my father and attempting, within the confines of our small flat, to do so without disturbing me, my younger brother and sister. She would attack him physically because he had again gambled away the week's wages in one of the many 'spielers' that abounded in the East End. Despite my mother's opprobrium and threats, gambling was something with which he persisted, sometimes with a degree of success, but mostly with failure, until the very day he died.

Woolfie would sometimes take me on his round delivering bread on the flatbed barrow to the various cafés in and around Cable Street and very occasionally to the Jewish Shelter that provided the main source of food for the ubiquitous poor, and to which my grandfather made regular and valuable contributions. It was his 'Mitzvah' that showed how generous a man he was and elevated him in the eyes of the Jewish community. His generosity gave him respect, and in turn he was blessed for it.

The cafés we delivered to were multi-ethnic; Maltese predominated but there was one for Asian seamen, another for Italian and several for the overwhelmingly Irish dockers. At the corner of Christian Street and Cable Street was the Cable Cinema. This was almost opposite Princes Square and convenient for my mother to use, and since my father, as a baker, worked nights, going to the cinema was her main cultural activity. We would be put to bed, and since there were three flats in the one building there was always someone willing to 'listen out' for any crying. In this event, my mother would be called prematurely from the cinema, but reassured by the manager that she could return the next day to see the part she'd missed!

When I was close to ten years old, my father decided to set up his own bakery business. I can only imagine that he had had 'a winning turn' and out of the monies he'd won retained sufficient to take over a recently vacated bakery, together with living accommodation at 417 Hackney Road in Bethnal Green. This new place offered comparative luxury to us at the time, and it also introduced me to the world of small business – a world where hard work was the dominating ethic. In a short while I graduated to making early morning deliveries myself to the local cafés before going on to school. The Empress Café, situated opposite Cambridge Heath Station, was my favourite and it was always busy. In winter the windows were all steamed up and the early morning workers, on their way to work, would be seated in cubicles for six or more, eating mountainous breakfasts. The staff there treated me well, regularly feeding me slices of bread with beef dripping, unknown to my mother, who retained some Kosher food rituals.

All or most of the family were involved in the business – survival was impossible without that input. Right from the moment we purchased the bakery, I was involved in making the evening batch of dough, even though I was still very young. My father, however, continued to gamble, restrained only by his lack of free time. Involving me in the bakery did though leave him free to visit the dogs, whist drives or a 'spieler'. After his little flutter, however tired he might be, he'd set to work, since in most bakeries a disproportionate amount of night work was obligatory, but it suited his lifestyle. My mother, too, despite her frequent pregnancies, worked long and arduous hours.

Until well into our teens, my siblings and I were compelled to be at my Morris grandparent's place every Sunday for tea. Always, as we approached No. 86 the big question in my mind and certainly in my mother's was: what kind of mood will aunt Stella be in? She was the archetypal 'when she was good she was very, very good but when she was bad she was horrid'. She was very competent at her work, though, having progressed from being a shorthand typist to become an all-round manager with a good knowledge of accountancy and bookkeeping. She took on numerous jobs, and from a very early age was prepared to move around to obtain the best positions and rewards, something not usual in those days. Unfortunately the rewards she expected included secretly paying herself a share of the profits. When this activity made her continued work for large, well known fashion magazines untenable, she made herself invaluable working for smaller organisations.

After a series of aborted engagements to various men, she was finally about to tie the knot with a bachelor of a similar age, from which one may deduce that he was also near to being remaindered on the shelf (or as my mother, more colourfully described him: 'an alter bock'). My grandfather was highly pleased with the prospect of her marriage, because he'd feared that she would for ever

A day out in Southend with Mum and Dad in 1921.

remain the Damocles sword hanging over him for the rest of his days. But to his horror, her then employer, who manufactured silk underwear and pyjamas, called on him one late evening just prior to the wedding and informed him that stock and monies were missing from the company coffers. He had only discovered this because my aunt had taken some days off to prepare for her wedding.

The old man, grandfather Alex Morris, for a number of reasons, including his reputation, but primarily to get my aunt off his back, scrounged from his friends to raise the necessary to prevent the police being informed and having to call off the wedding. It eventually took place and, despite the inauspicious beginning, blossomed into a successful and lasting marriage. And even at that late stage in their lives, the two of them managed to produce Dorrie, a lovely baby, who grew to become a highly intelligent young woman, but she unfortunately died a much too early death, very soon after Stella. This was doubly sad, because we had all hoped that free from the tyrannical restraints of her mother, she would have had many happy years ahead of her, but it was not to be.

Tea at my grandparents could be congenial but more often than not the occasion was characterised by argument and mutually exchanged ridicule. I was always amazed how grown men could argue so vigorously about how other people were incapable of running their businesses, yet were such dismal failures in running their own. Work matters dominated the male conversation.

Both my father and his brother Ruby had their own businesses and each was a craftsman at his trade, however, both were unable to control their gambling habits, for which their families suffered. My aunts had the habit of talking simultaneously across each other without giving way and the consequence was conversational bedlam. Opinions were bandied about aggressively but just as quickly shot down. '*You're* telling me?' they would yell, and 'What would *you* know?' in haughty disdain. These were the most over-used phrases I remember hearing during any discussion. Tumultuous floods of tears coupled with threats of never entering the house again were not an unusual culmination of such exchanges. Despite these acrimonious partings, though, come the following Sunday, all would be forgiven or forgotten, but in no time they would be at it again, hammer and tongs.

I remember the advent of the 'Wonderloaf' — the first sliced and wrapped white bread, the brainchild of American capitalist enterprise. It was claimed it would revolutionise the baking industry in Britain. In fact it did not so much revolutionise, as cause the eventual demise of thousands of small bakeries like my father's. The fact that it was 'pristine' white, sliced and hygienically wrapped was indeed different and made it seem desirable, but the bread itself was 'wet' — it was not so much baked as steamed. Taking advantage of the then greaseproof wrapping, the manufacturers found they could pump more water into the bread during the manufacturing process, thus making huge savings on flour. Similar methods were used later, and still are, to pump extra water into ham and other meats to increase their weight. In those days because the idea was unusual and not known here, there were no restrictions and no need even to list ingredients. The wonderful innovative ideas capitalism comes up with!

'It will never succeed', was the general consensus around our table, 'and in any case it won't affect us'. But it was a success, and with the backing of large millers, the small bakeries were driven to the wall. Of course, at that time, it was difficult for them to envisage such an eventuality. Who would have thought a decade or so back that a fast food outlet selling a fatty minced meat product in a soggy bun would dominate the high street as McDonalds does today? It was true, however, that it didn't affect small Jewish bakeries in the short term, since without fully realising it they were specialists with a niche market.

My mother's elder sister, Sarah lived close to us, both when we were in Cable Street and in Hackney Road. She would go down to the bakery on Friday afternoon with her own ingredients and, while the ovens were still hot, make her 'kichels' − little round biscuits to her own special recipe. She only used the baking sheets and the oven, working diligently and quietly. When it was baked and packed away, she would thank whoever was there, and then she was away.

When my grandfather was still alive they would take in 'chulants' at the Cable Street bakery, on Friday evenings from people in the area. This was after the ovens had cooled somewhat and the chulants would be left in the ovens until lunchtime on the Sabbath, when they would be ready cooked for the Sabbath meal. Usually done in large, high-sided, metal vessels, the chulant, in its various guises, could consist of a chunk of meat, usually flap or brisket, together with one or more large dumplings and potatoes, masses of various beans, all topped up with water. The chulants would be sealed, sometimes with brown paper, but more often with layers of newspaper. At the Hackney Road bakery we would do the same with turkeys. On the night before Christmas after the oven had been shut down people would bring them in and then collect them the next day.

My uncle Ruby was not dissimilar to my father in build and attitude to life but unlike his brother, he lost his first wife soon after their first child was born. Their son, Joe Morris, was then adopted by my grandmother Esther, but soon became the property of Stella and to a lesser degree Raie. It was they who ensured his education to matriculation standard, enabling him, later, to become a chartered accountant.

Unfortunately Joe's relations with Stella became more acrimonious as he grew older and all hell was let loose when, unbeknown to her and any other member of the family, he married Una, who was herself a somewhat difficult person and not dissimilar to Stella in temperament. As a result he was banned from her house.

Joe established himself in business and did well. Despite intermittent squab-
bles, recrimination and reconciliations with his aunt, he kept contact with the
family until in the mid 1930s he took a senior accounts position with a large corporation based in India where he served for a number of years, had a daughter,
Lea, and after finishing his term of office, returned to England. But the family
found it difficult to acclimatise and, a few months before the outbreak of the
Second World War, he accepted a similar position in Singapore. His family was
planning to follow him. Unfortunately, no sooner had he landed than the imminent threat of invasion by the Japanese meant that he was called up and made
an officer in the British Army. His career as an officer did not last long, for he
was very soon taken prisoner by the Japanese and forced to slave on the Burma
Road, under atrocious conditions of hunger, maltreatment and disease, until
Japan was eventually defeated. He returned home a very sick man, almost weight-
less and struggling to survive. He died as a consequence of this experience not
many years later.

Ruby, in the meantime, had his own baking business in Lower Chapman
Street off Watney Market near to Cable Street. He employed a young Catholic
girl, Nell Casey, as assistant in the shop, and they married, despite vigorous
objections from Nell's family, in particular her mother whom it was rumoured
chased Ruby all along Watney Market, threatening him with the vilest of deaths.
He got it in the neck from both sides, as he had thought it better not to inform
his own parents or siblings that his wife-to-be was not Jewish. They went on to
have six children, but Nellie died of tuberculosis at the age of 41. The eldest child,
Leslie, was in his early teens and the youngest were twin boys of not yet three
years old at the time. The twins and the youngest girl were placed in a children's
home and the burden of running the family home fell on the eldest girl, Doris,
who was then barely out of school.

The Chapman Street business later failed and Ruby eventually moved to the
Old Kent Road, opening a bakery next door to the fire station. He managed to
get the children back into his care, although the burden of this landed largely on
Doris. Despite his constant inability to sustain his business enterprises – the Old
Kent Road bakery failed as did successive attempts in other areas – the family
held together. Leslie went on to become an excellent baker and pastry cook, and
served in the Royal Artillery until his capture after being wounded at El Alamein.
He also spent the remainder of his time as a prisoner of war.

Doris met and married a young Scots serviceman, Neil King, and raised a
family of three girls and two boys. The last time I saw Ruby was shortly before
he died. I was driving my cab, in the early morning and approaching Claridges

Hotel, and there he was carrying bulging carrier bags, coming out of the employees' entrance after having spent the night baking the hotel's bread and rolls for that day. We had a long confab while I took him to the nearest underground for his journey back to his home in Tooting.

Alfie, another of Ruby's sons, served in the Navy, married Josie, with whom he had three daughters. The twins became apprenticed in the Joe Lyons scheme, spending some time in Switzerland but mostly at Cadby Hall. Before, during, and after the Second World War, Cadby Hall was an extensive complex of buildings in Kensington near where Olympia is now. It was owned by J. Lyons and Co. and each individual building was a production centre for specific items, like cakes or confectionary. In others the training of staff, including managers and chefs for their Corner House restaurants, took place. Lyons Corner Houses were spacious and often operated on several floors. You could obtain all kinds of reasonably-priced meals there, served at any time of the day, and one of their specialities was 'tea dances'. These Corner Houses were situated at Marble Arch, the Trocadero in Piccadilly, the Angel Islington, the corner of Tottenham Court Road and New Oxford Street. Each had a gypsy band comprised mainly of unemployed Jewish musicians from the East End, like my contemporary, Harry Gold, who became famous later with his Pieces of Eight band. In addition there were smaller premises serving teas and basic, but popular dishes such as eggs and beans on toast. Lyons also had restaurants in Olympia, and even had a school in Lucerne where they sent apprentices for training. Ruby's twins were both accepted as apprentices, as was Woolfie's son, Anthony. The business was owned by the Salmon and Gluckstein families. It all sank in the late nineteen seventies, when needs and tastes changed.

I was a reasonably intelligent pupil of Teasdale Street School, which I attended regularly, until I became overly fond of football. My urge to play whenever possible, combined with the pressures of working in the family business, may well have contributed to my failing the infamous ll-plus examination. Nevertheless I won a place at Central School, Mansford Street, and accepted it. I was unaware at the time, but the school was held in high academic esteem and offered real opportunities to its students, many of whom were there not because of failure, but due to the manipulative and pragmatic system used to decide which pupils would go to the Grammar, Central or Secondary schools.

My prowess at football grew in inverse proportion to my learning achievements, as did the increasing level of commitment to the family business. Although I enjoyed the atmosphere and the higher standard of teaching, I was compelled, by the demands of my father, to leave Mansford on the day before my fourteenth birthday. Two things happened at Mansford, which later played an important part in my life. Mr. Arkwright, a slightly built man, with a pinched face and a pencil-thin moustache, was for a time my teacher. He was a veteran of the First World War and the first socialist I had ever met. He was easily drawn by the pupils into telling us tales of the conflict. Some were about his own experiences in the 1914-18 war, but in the main they were of the horrors of war in general. He could be so easily diverted by us from the scheduled lesson. His advocacy of socialism was of necessity somewhat muted but sufficient to kindle my interest and curiosity. At that time a declaration of socialist convictions by a teacher would have been reason enough for dismissal.

Another person, cut from similar cloth, was Joe Morrison. The occasion I became aware of him was incongruous but remains a vivid memory. Joe was squatting under the shed in the playground. He was surrounded by a group of boys and girls, and was expounding to them the virtues of belonging to a trade union. Despite having a dreadful stammer, which he fought to overcome over many years and finally managed to do so, he could eloquently explain matters to them using the simplest examples. I was immediately drawn to him and we later became lifelong friends and socialists.

My weekday began with an early morning start. The family had acquired a box tricycle on which I was obliged to ride an ever-increasing mileage and with ever heavier loads. Despite this, our financial circumstances had not improved as a result of my father's intensified gambling. However, we were still better off than most of the families around us. True, we had bailiffs around so often, they could have been live-in lodgers, but at least we didn't lack bread to eat! Occasionally, of course, there would be a win, and my mother's rings would once again come out of pawn, the 'visitors' would disappear for a time and my father became more amenable.

Despite my commitments, I still found time for occasional football matches and played for Bethnal Green schoolboys and attended, for a very short time, Clapton Orient's juniors. Much to my father's chagrin, I also deepened my involvement in politics – a subject we never discussed – but then we hardly discussed anything anyway, not even work. As the boss he was entitled to complete obedience and, as my father, even more so. My relationship with him rapidly deteriorated as I grew up. By the time I reached eleven, I found myself the eldest of five children. My mother clearly didn't want any more and had already had more than one abortion, at a time when it was still illegal and dangerous. With a large family and the business, it meant that she worked incredibly long hours. Marrying my father was considered at the time by many to be a 'good catch', as my father was handsome and his parents were thought to be extremely wealthy. He was also a craftsman at his trade, something that promised security and a regular income. To my mother and her family, her marriage was like entering another world, in every sense. She was a beautiful woman, but she was also, as were most women of her background and era, very dutiful in terms of what were generally accepted as marriage obligations.

My maternal family was gentle, industrious, sober and generous. Probably this was one of the reasons the Morris family was allowed to dominate our lives. Times at home were characterised by the long hours culture imposed by the bakery, and domestic arguments. However there were moments of pleasure which I recall with relish. Very occasional visits to the nearby Hackney Empire, where I saw many of the top music hall artists of the day – Lily Morris, Gus Ellen, Vesta Victoria, Marie Lloyd and Harry Champion – became an addiction for me. Later in life, I went as often as my meagre finances allowed. I also became a frequent habitué of the pit at the Holborn Empire and in the 'Gawds' at the London Palladium. In much later years I would take my father to performances there, but he never showed the exuberant appreciation that I did; he would always recall some performer from the old days who was better. His favourite over all the years was the 'Polutski Brothers', a duo who, in his eyes and memory, could out-perform even Flanagan and Allen. Flanagan no doubt earned his admiration particularly because, as a Jewish comic from London's East End, he was also noted for his gambling. I always imagined the 'Brothers' to be a figment of his imagination, mentioned to discredit any appreciation I might express for modern performers. Many years later when visiting the Players' Theatre in Villiers Street, in the Strand, I almost exploded with laughter when I indeed saw their names up there among all the other old-timers displayed on the safety curtain.

My maternal grandparents were ultra-orthodox. This was not surprising, since my grandfather, originally a cobbler, but now unable to work at his trade, became a teacher of Hebrew. He had no designated synagogue which would have given him a remuneration of sorts, so was dependent on a limited number of pupils, who ensured only a meagre income. He lived with his wife in two tiny rooms in the grandly-named Rothschild Mansions on the corner of Flower and Dean Street, off Commercial Street. It was an elongated building with a central square. There were entrances to and from Flower and Dean Street as well as from Thrawl Street. Their tiny kitchen was situated virtually on the landing. These 'mansions' were a large block of cheap dwellings built to accommodate the influx of working class Jews from Eastern Europe at the turn of the century. It had previously been a slum area inhabited by the poor, the hungry, the thieves and the prostitutes who had been drawn to the dockland area of East London, until the land was bought by Jewish benefactors.

Nearby was Wentworth Street, part of Petticoat Lane market. My uncle

Barney, the younger of my mother's elder brothers had a small barber's shop in Thrawl Street, which soon became the central place to catch up on the area's male gossip. He it was who gave all young members of the family their very first haircuts. As youngsters, we would sit on a plank of wood he placed across the arms of the chair, which allowed us to sit higher, so that he wouldn't have to bend so much. His ability to listen without passing opinion made him the ideal receptacle for gossip and stories; so very different from anyone else in the Morris family, most of whom were avid talkers. Barney, despite his taciturnity, had a ready wit, and these qualities made him very popular and this was an invaluable asset in his business.

CHAPTER THREE
From bar mitzvah to Bethnal Green Library

My maternal grandfather taught me my bar mitzvah. He was a gentle person, a quality I found most welcome since my previous teachers had been out and out sadists, particularly a Mr. Fabrican who wielded the cane as if it were permanently attached to the end of his arm. My grandfather appeared to me to be very old and frail. He had snow-white hair, a moustache and beard, both heavily stained with nicotine from the cigarette that hung permanently from his mouth. He used an ivory pointer that was also heavily nicotine stained. He shuffled along on two sticks, yet managed to travel long and difficult distances to fulfil the commitments he had made. Easily, and without rancour he discussed with me my growing adolescent rebellion and anti-religious feelings. He made me feel as though my arguments were fresh and had never been put to him before. His sensitive and sympathetic manner was essential if he was to have any chance of overcoming my constant avowals of disbelief. He had, somewhat foolishly I felt, volunteered for the exacting task of trying to educate me. Only much later could I appreciate his adroitness and skill in handling my cussed approach to the whole business.

He disappeared from my life following my bar mitzvah; I was too heavily involved with my own pursuits to maintain the contact, and with the death of his wife, about whom I knew very little and can hardly remember, he moved some distance away to live with his eldest son, my uncle Hymie. I never made the journey to him that he had travelled so conscientiously and regularly for me, and this I regret, for he was easily the least bigoted religious man I have ever met.

The bar mitzvah is an important religious ceremony and ritual in which boys

Bar Mitzvah boy, 1932.

when thirteen years of age attain manly status through reading a section of the Torah in the synagogue on a Sabbath morning. This they have rehearsed possibly over a whole year or more. Being successful, the boy/young man, would be showered with 'Roshenkas mit mundlan' (raisins and almonds) and receive expressions of goodwill, coupled with manly handshakes and whiskery kisses from all the bearded male relatives and, much more pleasantly, pressed to the usually ample bosoms of the women in the family, which – intended or otherwise – suggested the promise of future erotic pleasures in this new man's world.

Another part of the ritual would be the gifts of numerous fountain pens, bringing to mind the perennial start to the boy's speech of "Now I am a fountain pen".

Up to, and until a short time after my bar mitzvah, I was compelled to attend one of my paternal grandfather's 'Shuls'. Although I was barmitzvahed at the Hambro Synagogue in Adler Street, I more often attended the one in Cannon Street over which Canon Halter presided. My indifference to prayer was compounded when, having walked about five miles to get there, so as not to compromise myself in the eyes of the devout, I found myself surrounded by the local boxing fraternity: Jack Solomons and Victor Berliner, competing promoters, various bookmakers and six-rounders, past and present, in a hushed discussion, which they didn't let the ongoing service disrupt.

Other members of my mother's extended family left Latvia for the United States, but, strangely, little to no contact had been maintained with them over the years, until very recently when the advent of the Internet facilitated a growing interest in genealogy. A spirited young American discovered that there were many Sidlin families scattered around the world, but principally in America where there were two strains: the Sidlins and the Sidlines. Attempts were made to hold a reunion in Florida, but unfortunately it was foreshadowed by the September 11th bombing of the twin towers. We were given to understand that there were also a large number of descendants spread across the States as well as quite a few in Argentina, Australia, Canada, Scandinavia and even one line in Japan.

My uncle Davis, aunt Sarah's husband, was an underpresser in a clothing factory. His job was to press the different parts of a garment before it was sewn together. He was over six feet tall and beneath his cloth cap he was completely bald. They moved from Fieldgate Street in Stepney to Scawfell Street, off Hackney Road, soon after we'd moved to Hackney Road, so he was close enough for me to visit, which I did, mostly on Saturday afternoons after synagogue. With his spectacles pushed up on his forehead, he was always absorbed in a book. These were always in Yiddish, although he spoke perfect English. He read the classics while, his wife, auntie Sarah, devoutly read the bible.

Bethnal Green Library at that time had shelves of books in Yiddish and Whitechapel Library had an even larger collection that he used regularly. It was from my uncle that I was introduced to writers like Dostoyevsky and Carlyle, Pushkin and Dickens, Thackeray, Mark Twain and Emile Zola. Strangely, he was also an ardent addict of Sherlock Holmes and particularly fond of the exploits of Moriarty, about which he'd expound to me at great length. Sometimes we met in the library and he'd suggest books for me to read and encourage me to become a registered reader. My moments with him were about the only contact with a higher literary culture that I had at that time. My taste in reading, of course, developed with the years but was always in a sense eclectic, and wide-ranging, tips culled from various sources were satisfied by using the excellent facility of Bethnal Green Library. I remember from among the many: W.W. Jacobs' *The Monkey's Paw,* James Hanley's *The Furies'*– the saga of an Irish Family – and J.M. Farrell's *Studs Lonnigan.* There were also, later, *Mansfield Park* and books by Conrad, a writer my uncle regarded very highly. It was a strange relationship between the two, a Jewish immigrant worker from Poland and the Polish-born writer, whose parents were landed aristocrats, but who wrote all his works in excellent English.

I vividly remember, even now, the opening chapters of Conrad's *Lord Jim.* The description of the sea and the ships and the men who crewed them were absolutely exhilarating and opened up a completely new world for me. My introduction to political novels came later, particularly those written by Upton Sinclair, like *The Jungle* and then, more importantly, Jack London's *The Iron Heel,* in which the arguments about the merits and demerits of capitalism and socialism were discussed in a down to earth language that I could relate to. It was similar with Robert Tressell's classic work, *The Ragged Trousered Philanthropists.* I suppose I was a romantic even back then, as I was totally enthralled by William Morris's utopian fantasy, *News from Nowhere.*

After Joe Morrison, my school-mate, and I had become serious friends he lent me an American novel by George Marlen called *The Road.* This novel was similar to Jack London's *The Iron Heel,* but had a clearer and more extensive explanation of the kind of society I had begun to dream of. It was these two books, with their straightforward explanation of society's ills and their uncomplicated and informative vision of a more humane and just future that made the greatest impressions on me. I borrowed and read *The Road* so often that it became like a bible to me.

On my demob from army service, years later, I borrowed it from Joe once again, but sadly it was becoming the worse for wear. I treasured it so much, though, that I had it rebound at my own expense before returning it to Joe. In later years, when I visited New York, I spent long sessions at Strand Books on 8th Street, in the hope that among their tremendous selection of second hand books I would find a copy, but I never did.

I have little remembrance of books in our own home, and I was the first of my siblings to become a reader. On the other hand, however, the enjoyment of performance was with us from an early age. During the thirties, each year near Christmas time, aunt Stella would take all the younger children in the family – no less than twenty of us, but most of the time closer to thirty – to see Bertram Mills's, world famous circus at Olympia. After which she would shepherd us into

Lyons's Cadby Hall restaurant for tea, where we would all be seated at one long table. Many a waitress, or 'nippies' as they were known, suffered the whiplash of her tongue, if the youngest were not provided with a highchair or a pillow to raise them to table height. Stella, with her assumed aristocratic airs, was nevertheless extremely generous most of the time, but could also be very difficult.

The People's Palace in Mile End Road occasionally had repertory theatre and it was there that we saw Edward G. Robinson as *The Amazing Doctor Clitterhouse* in the play of the same name. It had been successful during its London production but had flopped on Broadway. Later it was made into a film with Robinson as the Doctor and Humphrey Bogart as one of the heavies. Robinson in his early years had performed in Yiddish theatre in the USA as had Paul Muni, who also appeared at one time at the Pavilion Theatre in London.

Lily's mother Fanny had once travelled with a group of Yiddish actors she joined in Romania when in her teens, to escape an arranged marriage to an elderly widower with several children. She eventually came with them to London where the troupe split up. She married Philip Weinberg, a spindle hand, who worked in a woodwork factory. It was a trade noted for the damage done to workers' fingers and hands. Lily's dad died as a consequence of losing several fingers while working in that wood factory. His last accident caused him to have a heart attack, which proved fatal.

In my teens, when I was courting Lily, my future wife, we both came under the influence of my aunt Raie, who being a very modern young woman was a great reader and theatre patron. She was a member of the PEN Club that provided members with a number of free or heavily discounted tickets to West End theatres, and she would often pass tickets on to us. She was also a member of the seemingly exclusive library operated by Boots the chemist (there was a membership fee and a charge for loaning books) and she would recommend modern novels to me.

My auntie Raie left St.Georges High School in Cable Street to be among the first young women to enter Pitman's, the newly established school for secretaries. She was following her elder sister, Stella, who had previously taken up a course offered at that school and, from an early age, was able to establish herself in the world of commerce.

Raie, having finished her training, took a position as a junior at Pinchin Johnson, the paint people, which was a subsidiary of Docker Brothers. She remained with them until she was 51 years of age – a period of 38 years. During the war years she would help her friend who, with her husband, was a licensee of the Chequers pub in Duke of York street, off Jermyn Street in London's West End. This pub, like so many in its time, became a rendezvous for particular overseas servicemen; in this instance, Antipodeans, South Africans and Canadians. She was very popular there and made staunch friendships among the customers, many of whom left their addresses with her, offering a warm welcome if she ever visited their home countries. They also continued to communicate after the war was over.

Her decision to leave her employment was prompted by the promise contained in these offers; the romantic stories and descriptions of beautiful countries they told her and which she vividly retained. However, the normal passenger steamship route was not for her. She considered that would not give her the flexibility she desired, so she booked with a freighter line. These ships carried no more than 12 passengers normally in very good to excellent conditions. This way she would have a number of days on shore while the ships' cargoes were unloaded and reloaded when necessary, at ports en route. If she found a stop congenial, she would then stay on until the next ship arrived. If necessary she would work wherever and whenever it became essential, and with her universal skills this was easy.

Finally she reached Brisbane in Eastern Australia where her elder brother, my uncle Marks, was living. Marks was, like my father, a craftsman baker and also an obsessive gambler. So much so that he got into serious debt with the local bookie who was threatening him with serious consequences. Unmarried and without ties he fled and became a baker for a major steamship company. Docking at Brisbane, he had decided to try his luck miles from his burden of debt. He found work in a bakery in the town that was owned by a Catholic widow who was having some difficulty running the business and bringing up her eight children. He solved the first problem, but compounded the second by impregnating her with a daughter – providing the excuse for them to get married.

Raie stayed with her brother for little more than a year, finally deciding to move on, when one morning while reading a shared newspaper, she lifted her head and remarked that the news was terrible. She was referring to the Korean war. He mumbled agreement, but only because his mind was elsewhere – on the favourite in the forthcoming Melbourne Cup which had been withdrawn. This was enough for her. She suddenly realised the huge gap between them, and decided to move on.

She travelled on to New Zealand and then Fiji for a lengthy stay and a brief love affair. She then arrived in Vancouver, anticipating a stay of no more than two days, before proceeding by rail to Toronto, but she was so fascinated by the city that she stayed and worked there for six months before she finally left to visit her cousin Walter, the son of my great uncle Isaac, and owner of the fish and chip shop in Cable Street. From here she moved on to Chicago, where a friend was now living and where she stayed until her return home almost ten years later.

In Chicago she worked all the years for an International Welfare Foundation based in that city. She made many friends, all of whom became ours too. Whenever they were travelling to Britain they were told to contact us and we would make them welcome.

While my aunty Raie was in the United States she made many friends, and among them were Gisella and Al Booth, who came over several times to visit. Gisella was one of the Kindertransport children who escaped from Nazi Germany and had spent some time in England until she went on to relatives in Chicago. Al was a real estate salesman – an estate agent employee – mostly big stuff. During the seventies they came to London for a longer period and contemplated staying here. They rented a house in South London and soon made many friends among their neighbours.

One Christmas their immediate neighbours asked if they would like to join them at their local church where they were participating in a 'Do It Yourself Messiah'. Everyone in the congregation, together with their friends were invited to participate, whether they could sing or not, or were proficient in playing a musical instrument or not. Music and words were provided. Both Gisella and Al were musical and they joined in vigorously. Al became obsessed with this experience and decided they would return home and try doing something similar there.

Al is not the bashful type – he never missed an opportunity to push an idea or an acquaintance. He finally got it under way, but not in a church hall. In October 1977, the Chicago Symphony Hall was the venue for one night only. A minimal programme of advertising sold all the tickets in days and on the night there were crowds waiting outside in the snow hoping against hope that they could in some way participate. It was phenomenal – all religions and the various racial groups embraced it, making it an enormous success. The following year the evening was repeated with an extra performance. It was broadcast on public service radio and TV, and is still on going strong today.

This put Al into a new world and his mind began whirling with ideas. He had heard of the Myra Hess recitals that took place in London throughout the bombing, during the Second World War. Following the declaration of war against Germany on September 3rd all theatres, cinemas, concert halls and museums were closed. Three weeks later, Myra Hess, at that time one of the world's greatest pianists, persuaded the government to allow her to start a daily noon-day recital series at the National Gallery, where all the paintings and sculptures had already been removed for safe keeping. She opened the first concert in the series herself on October 10th 1939 and it was a great success. The concerts continued for five and a half years and enabled young musicians to perform on a fairly regular basis. This made a huge difference both for the public and for the performers, who often went on to become well know performers. Myra Hess was made a Dame of the British Empire. She died on November 25th 1965 leaving her entire estate to benefit young artists, stipulating that performances take place anywhere in the United Kingdom other then in major cities.

Al first encountered these later concerts at the Bishopsgate Institute Library and St. James' Church in Piccadilly, and it was the idea of providing a platform for young artists that preoccupied him. On October 20th 1977, the first of the Chicago Dame Myra Hess Memorial Concerts took place in the magnificently restored Bradley Preston Hall of the newly reopened Chicago Public Library Cultural Centre, under the sponsorship of the Talman Home Federal Savings and Loan Association. Since then the concerts have been presented free of charge, each week before live audiences of up to 500. In addition, these concerts are broadcast over the main Chicago radio station and in more than 500 affiliated satellite stations across the United States.

Al made contact with Yehudi Menuhin, who was deeply involved in assisting young artists in Britain and Europe, and he agreed to co-operate in an exchange of artists. Among the extraordinary number of young musicians to have benefited from such exchanges are Nigel Kennedy and more recently one of our premier harpsichord musicians, Maggie Cole. Others were recommended by Alfred Brendel, Claudio Abbado and Leonard Slatkin. Many came from the international competitions held all over the world.

The cooperation with Menuhin encouraged Booth to start a series of Live Music Now performances in Chicago. This is a programme of concerts of both classical and modern music within the state schools and are available free of charge for all grades. Today in Chicago the tradition of Dame Myra Hess continues each week under the present sponsorship of La Salle Bank. They are coordinated by the International Music Federation, of which Al is the founder and now president, together with the Department of Cultural Affairs and the Chicago Public Library. The Foundation's mission is to make the arts available to everyone.

Lily's mother, Fanny, was left a widow with seven children, living in two rooms above what was a bag-wash laundry on the corner of Old Nichol Street and Chance Street. Without washing machines, families had to resort to putting their dirty washing in hessian sacks and taking them to the local laundry. The washing came back heavily bleached and very wet and so, as each garment was removed, it had to be shaken vigorously with considerable strength and stamina. Then of course there was the drying problem; the clothes would be hung out wherever possible − in the backyard or on the balconies of the buildings and often indoors on lengths of string, stretching wall to wall, or on large clothes' horses, in front of the open fire.

Fanny's life was still the Yiddish Theatre, which flourished in the East End, both at the Grand Palais in Commercial Road and at the Pavilion Theatre, which soon increasingly became an important venue for professional boxing, then extremely popular with young Jews because of the recent success of several Jewish fighters. The Pavilion, at its zenith, though, had produced classical plays in Yiddish by Shakespeare and also the Russian giants like Chekhov.

The family lived close to where the Boundary Estate is now, and it was once one of the most infamous and notorious areas of London, known as The Jago. It was the resort of thieves, murderers, prostitutes and rogues of all sorts. In its heyday there was only one way into its labyrinthine network of streets and alleyways, through Boundary Passage which is still there and with the same pub on the corner. In his book 'Children of The Jago', J. J. Morrison describes in great detail the terrible lives its inhabitants endured there.

Lily and I would occasionally go with her mother to the Grand Palais that was somewhat downmarket of the Pavilion Theatre. Love stories, melodrama and musicals were the norm, and the plays, no matter the genre, always induced tears. The story line invariably involved a beautiful girl, a villain and thwarted love.

The seating consisted of ordinary kitchen chairs, and without exception there would be Yiddish speakers in the audience loudly translating for one or more companions unable to understand the English or who were too hard of hearing. Then of course there were those, who were unable to separate real life from acted drama, who participated by sobbing loudly, or shouting instructions to the hero/heroine on how to avoid disaster or betrayal. The singing was usually of an acceptably high standard, but the dancing – 'oy gervalt!' – was both unorthodox and surreal, with the constant danger of the stage collapsing under the dancers' weight.

During the Second World War, on the 14th June 1943, a story appeared in the *Daily Express* that a Jewish man, Sidney Cohen, a 23 year old tailors' cutter from East London, turned sergeant gunner in the RAF, whose plane had landed unintentionally on an island in the Mediterranean, had personally accepted the Italian surrender. He became known as The King of Lampedusa. Out of this incident was born the play of the same name, written by Shmuel Charendorf, and when it was put on, it featured Yudl Goldberg in the name part and the very popular Myer Tzelnicker and his daughter Anna taking the other two leading parts. There were lengthy queues, and the play had the longest run of any previously performed at the theatre.

Always, when we accompanied Fanny, she would meet up with her thespian friends and they would talk shop, being also highly critical of the dramas we saw. I remember one of these actresses, a Mrs. Pottesman, who had clearly been quite a beauty in her younger days. Her favourite performance piece was a Yiddish version of 'Goodbye Dolly Grey', which according to Fanny, always brought the house down, as she marched across the stage in a highly decorative First World War uniform, inside which her voluptuously rounded body was provocatively encased. She eventually married a wealthy admirer, one of her many stage door 'Johnies'. With her increased wealth and position, her main concern, apart from ageing, became her weight. Her husband, though, remained her greatest admirer and had a business in the classier end of the 'Shmutter game' − dressmaking. He devised a strategy for his wife of which no one was supposed to be aware: all the dresses he made for her were of stretchable material! The first words that came from her lips, uttered in her theatrical Yiddish, upon greeting her friends would be: 'Look, how thin I am.' At the same time she would playfully grasp the dress and pull the cloth it to its limits.

CHAPTER FOUR
From cinema high drama to murder in the kitchen

We had no live music in our house but we were fortunate to have a rented radio, at least from when I was in my very early teens. When, on the rare occasions my younger brother Teff and I were allowed to stay up really late, we would listen to the broadcasts of Lew Stone and his orchestra from the Monsignor Restaurant and similarly Henry Hall and his BBC orchestra, as well as Roy Fox and Ambrose with their big bands. We became acquainted with the overweight drummer, Max Bacon and his rendering of songs with a strong Jewish accent. We also listened to Al Bowley, Hutch, Adelaide Hall, Leayton and Johnson and many others. It was through the radio that I received my introduction to modern music. I would listen and try to imagine what it was like to be wearing evening dress, with a glamorous woman on my arm and dining on exotic foods. It was possible to do this in our heads, helped by the glamorous lives we lived vicariously through the cinema. Of course it was absolute fantasy, but the music was real and the tunes reverberated in my head, so that I was always whistling one of them as I went about my daily chores.

My very first cinema visit was to see Lon Chaney in *West of Zanzibar* at the Standard Cinema in Goldsmith Row. It was a sub-titled, silent film with accompanying music played live by a pianist in the pit. I recall the lady pianist playing particularly stirring music in one scene where native Africans danced round a fire. And this piece of music stayed with me long after the film's images had faded. Only much later did I learn that it was *In the Hall of the Mountain Kings*, from Grieg's *Peer Gynt Suite*.

I was about twelve when I took Teff, my brother, and Jean, the eldest of my sisters, to see our first talkie. It was the *Jazz Singer* with Al Jolson. We arrived back home afterwards with eyes raw from crying and wet pants. There were numerous cinemas close to our home in those days. The Smart, in Bethnal Green Road, was one of the first to be built, then there was The Foresters in Cambridge Heath Road, built on the site of the Poor Law Institute. The London in Shoreditch High Street was a music hall before its brief transformation into a cinema.

Len Lermer was a school friend, whose parents agreed to have a billboard outside their shop that advertised the variety programme at the London Theatre. The reward for this was two free seats each week. During a performance which Len attended, and excitedly told me about afterwards, the shoulder strap of one of the chorus girls snapped and, according to Len, he had a full frontal view of her breasts, nipples and all! As normal, frustrated adolescents, we marvelled and envied him this experience

The opening of the Troxy cinema in Commercial Road, Stepney introduced a fresh concept. For our sixpence we could see both an A and a B film with a regular orchestra, an organist and three top-line variety performers. The resident organist was Bobby Pagan and there would be complete silence before his performance, during which the magnificent organ would rise up from the depths. Teddy Joyce introduced a resident 'boys' band' of exceptional quality and the other artists were also of a high standard. It was there I saw Wilson, Kepple and Betty, a sand dance act with an Egyptian theme and exotic music to go with it. And on one occasion we experienced the fabulous Four Mills Brothers. This was just after one of them died and had to be replaced by their father.

On most Saturdays a close friend, Sammy Hyman, would get a picnic from his mother and he would go to the Troxy Cinema at midday and, since the programmes were continuous, he would sit through as many performances as possible until he was made to leave. You always had to queue for the cinema in the thirties, as it was the main entertainment for working people, and while queuing we would be entertained by a variety of buskers. This was also the custom outside theatres in the West End. In earlier days there had been Old Solomon Levy, the very first one-man band, equipped with a huge drum on his back, cymbals on the inside of his thighs, a mouth organ and a loud but fluttering voice giving rendition to his self-composed songs, all of which extolled the virtues of himself, 'Old Solomon Levy'. But the most intriguing acts for me were the transvestite dancers who, backed by a barrel organ, and dressed in ornate but scruffy dresses, would entertain with song and dance. Alongside all this, there would be the toffee man, who peddled home made toffees from a barrow. He had a large variety, all in trays, and would crack the toffee with a short flat-headed hammer and

wrap it either in cones made of newspaper or, for the more affluent of his customers, in small brown bags which hung from a hook on the barrow.

Apart from the cinema, there was a whole range of variety and musical acts
to choose from. These would include a very professional imitation of the afore-
mentioned Wilson, Keppel and Betty, a tattooed man who swallowed razor
blades, an excellent accordionist, several singers, good, bad and indifferent, tap
dancers impersonating the then popular Jack Buchanan, and the inevitable
escapologist.

We were a very varied group of Jewish families who lived in the area and our
parents practised a whole number of trades and skills, but we had our own separate aspirations. There were those whose parents could afford, or who struggled
to afford, to send their sons (rarely their daughters) to better schools − if they
didn't pass the ll-plus − or pay for coaching. Those, like Percy Tours, whose
father was an outworking tailor, were introduced at an early age to the machinations, the deadlines and harsh conditions set by the company employing his family. Percy could be seen regularly shouldering a black sack filled with work for the
'shop', scurrying along struggling under the heavy load; he was a little lad, but
never walked. He went on to become a tailor just like his father. Len Lerner's
father was an outworker making caps and hats, and he was always called on to
work excessive hours during the 'season'. There was always a season in tailoring
− for a few months each year everything was urgent and long tedious hours were
worked, then there would be little or nothing for the rest of the year.

One of our friends became an accountant and spent most of his working life
with the Jewish Board of Guardians. My own younger brother Teff, who did pass
the ll-plus was allowed priority time for studying before doing more mundane
chores which we all had to do. A rare exception to all of us was Cookie Bernstein
who suddenly decided he wanted to be a musician and made only occasional
efforts to belong to our group. He could be heard almost every evening practising his concertina. He became Tito Burns who, with his band, became quite successful before becoming a theatrical agent.

Other youngsters of my age went into cabinet making, tailoring or to the
Houndsditch Warehouse Company in Middlesex Street, where they trained literally thousands as salesmen, particularly in menswear. My own cousin, Joe Sidlin,
whose father (my mother's brother), as I already mentioned, was the community
barber for the residents of the 'mansions' around Thrawl Street, followed in his
father's footsteps. But his secret ambition had always been to become an opera
singer. While he never realised his dreams, he did manage some passable solos
as Don José in Don Rico's band of 'Magyar gypsies' (the band consisted large-

ly of similarly frustrated musicians from East London) that appeared regularly on bandstands at seaside resorts in the South of England

This generation of my friends from those early days were, in the main, the first in their families to have received a full time education. It produced not only craftsmen in the various trades, but also medical doctors like Bennie Hyman, a number of teachers, an optician and a radio technician. Jack Nissen, the radio technician, served in Special Services during the war and was awarded the highest Canadian military award for bravery. Most of us, of course, were later to serve in the war, and some of us never returned.

As school children, our domain was the area of Teasdale Street from Bethnal Green Road to Old Bethnal Green Road and the parallel Blythe Street. A large group of us would congregate on the corner of Weare Street to the despair of Mr Nemko who owned the grocery shop there. But as we became more aware of girls, we drifted towards the Boundary Estate in Shoreditch where they seemed to be more plentiful and in greater variety. This entailed a walk through the bustling market that was strung out along one side of Bethnal Green Road, its stalls offering all kinds of goods, but predominantly food.

On winter evenings the spitting kerosene lamps would light up the bloodied corpses of gutted rabbits hung on hooks from the roofs, and often we would linger fascinated by the eels writhing in long trays, until they were cut into small pieces, each of which continued writhing until cooked. I was also intrigued by the sweet makers. They would boil sugar and water, adding flavourings and colour. These were then mixed and the gooey mass slung onto large butcher's hooks to be pulled into long strands, then hooked back up time and time again until the mass became a long, elastic and translucent 'rope'. This rope would be laid on a greased slab, rolled into ever increasing lengths and then chopped with a pair of special scissors into small, four cornered pieces and other shapes to make still-warm, delectable sweets – either humbugs, Everton mints or peppermint knobs. One such favourite was a stick made up of three thin orange-coloured strands twisted together and cut into six-inch strips, tasting strongly of aniseed; they were the cause of my first impulse buying.

There were many markets like the Bethnal Green one throughout the East End. Roman Road market was nearby, as was the Brick Lane one, which unlike the others, catered more for Jewish people and was really a much smaller version of and an adjunct to the larger and world renowned one of Petticoat Lane. Before we moved to Hackney Road, my favourite market was Hessel Street, off the Commercial Road, where I would accompany my mother to buy Kosher chickens from shops stacked with crates of live, plump chickens which, unlike the supermarket chickens of today, had never seen battery cages, but had enjoyed a life in the open and a choice of feed. In these places the smell of death always lingered, as the warm corpses of the chickens were examined and flung around indiscriminately and indifferently while being hand-weighed, pressed and pushed during the process of decision-making, which was done mostly by women who always surrounded the stalls, like a flock of flapping crows. In a room behind the stalls, a small group of women could be seen plucking the feathers off the dead birds. While I found the sight and smell here nauseous, my revulsion was soon overcome by the culinary glory of a roasted bird or my mother's chicken soup, which tasted deliciously and succoured my growing frame.

It was a similar situation with the fish. At Ruda's, on the other side of the street, there was a large tank fixed to the wall in which live fish, mostly carp and bream, swam, seemingly indifferent to their imminent fate – becoming a dish of gefilta fish on the family's Sabbath table. The fishmonger would net the chosen one and deftly deal it a deadly blow to the head and almost immediately it would be either filleted, which was rare in those days, or its scaly sides cleaned and the fish sliced into cutlets of the desired size.

I have never understood why, my father once decided that he would purchase two live fish and deal with them at home. Whether this was to avoid any extra charge for the work entailed in its preparation, I could not be sure. Nevertheless when he brought the fish back to the house, they were first put into a Butler sink, which were always deeper than normal. When my younger siblings had seen enough of the swimming monsters, he decided it was time to play the executioner. What a hilarious yet sickening disaster it was! They were very slippery and, sensing their impending demise, jumped and twisted for dear life, flip-flopping out of my father's grip and then flapping around on the kitchen floor, gasping for air, creating an enormous hullabaloo, before he was able to finally finish the job. But after all that rigmarole, no one could face eating the resultant dish and my father was not best pleased!

CHAPTER FIVE
Early political awakenings

I became conscious of the hypocrisy of our governments and the inhumanity of the plutocracy from very early on in my life. The basics of my political education and development came about as a consequence of experiencing the effects of the economic depression on the community all around me during my youth.

Welsh miners came to the area to sing in the streets for a few pennies; grown men and older boys would hang around all day long on street corners, devoid of hope; some of them had been at school with me. Women knocked on the door, asking for yesterday's bread so that they could feed their children, and little kids begged for broken biscuits.

Fixed to the wall in Dinmont Street, as on the walls of many other streets, lined by those mean and tiny terraced houses, was a small plaque with the names of the men from the immediate area killed in the 1914-18 war. Attached to the plaque was a small metal tube. And the fact that it usually containing only a few limp and faded flowers seemed to indicate that the pressures of present survival outweighed painful memories of the recent past.

In almost every home there would be photographs of proud men in uniform – husbands and sons in their tens of thousands who never returned from the battle-fields of northern France and Belgium. More and more I began to question the logic of all this senseless waste of human potential; it created in me a strong sense of social injustice that I've never lost.

Health care and access to medicines was expensive when I was growing up, which was before the establishment of our National Health Service by Nye Bevan in 1949. Good treatment was well beyond the means of ordinary people. There were, though, saving associations and insurances for those that could afford it, but for the poor and unemployed there was only charity and the poor house on Cambridge Heath Road.

As small children at Teasdale Street School we were taken one day to see, and to cheer, the Prince of Wales who opened The Hospital for Sick Children in Hackney Road. He arrived in an open car and we showed due deference by lining the roads, waving our small Union Jacks and cheering. At the same time there came into focus a man riding a white horse which distracted my attention. Seated upon this beast was a well known, and in most quarters highly regarded, local doctor. There was no tangible relationship between the two images but I can still remember thinking how it was that they were who they were and what connection they had with me, just little me.

With the assistance of the East End History Society, I learned much later that the doctor was Henry Percy Jelley who opened his practice in Hackney in 1910. In 1911, at the age of 45 he married 17 year-old Florence Glenham after a whirlwind romance and expanded his work setting up several surgeries, but very soon had legal problems because of his, apparently, rather unorthodox treatment of patients. He was probably one of those doctors who was prepared to flout the law for extra money and carry out abortions or offer other irregular services. In 1916 he was charged with the murder of Caroline Marsh, who died following such an abortion, and was sentenced to three years imprisonment, but released during the Spanish flu epidemic after serving only two years. Although struck off, he continued to treat patients from his surgery above a grocery store on the corner of Hackney Road and Lawrence Street. He was known as the 'Threepenny Doctor' and his surgery was well supported by the impoverished for whom he was the cheapest source of medical care. He was, though, constantly harassed by the police and in perpetual conflict with his neighbours and even some patients. Nevertheless I heard of visits made to him by my mother and our neighbours and he was well remembered for his charity and kindnesses. He died soon after the end of the Second World War. He was born in 1866 in Totnes, Devon, later married and had two sons, but became a widower in 1909. He passed his final medical exams in Glasgow and qualified as a medical practitioner in 1910.

Lily recalls her visits as a child to the Mildmay Mission near where she lived and where you could see a doctor or nurse free of charge provided you were prepared to join in the regular sessions of hymn singing.

I learned to drive soon after leaving school. One of my friends was Bert Copsey whose father worked for the removal firm of Sullys. His family lived above the offices of the firm in Hackney Road and garaged the company's three T-type Ford Luton style vans at the bottom of Dinmont Street. We were both allowed to drive the vehicles down the road and into the garage. After a while we were allowed to drive local distances and I became well acquainted with motors and how they worked. Not so long after this experience, my father purchased a small Jowett Javelin two-stroke van that he also let me drive. However, we had the car for only a short while until it was reclaimed by the hire purchase people because of non-payment. But it gave me valuable driving experience and when I became seventeen, and compulsory driving tests had been introduced, I easily obtained a licence.

In the thirties the frightening news from Europe began filtering through from Germany and Austria about the seemingly inevitable rise of fascism and the perse-cution of socialists, communists, the Jews and other minorities. The rise of Nazism in mainland Europe also found its echo and adherents here in Britain. The British Union of Fascists under Oswald Mosley's leadership introduced the uniformed marches and political violence to the streets of the East End. In the next block to where we lived there was a small greengrocer's run by Italian immigrants, Mr and Mrs Leoni. We had friendly and polite relations with them for years until we saw their two adult sons strutting around in full Italian fascist regalia. Although then only 13, I became very quickly and heavily involved in opposing the rise of fascism and have continued to do so throughout my life.

Despite warnings from the League of Nations, Italy's fascist leader, Benito Mussolini, invaded the desperately poor country of Abyssinia (now Ethiopia and Eritrea), whose inhabitants were obliged, failing help and support from the interna-tional community, to confront the well equipped and trained Italian army with spears and a few ancient rifles. On 2nd October 1935 the Italians invaded and by April of the following year, after heavy bombing and terrible massacres of virtually unarmed civilians, Haile Selassie the Emperor, fled to Palestine and Mussolini declared his own monarch the new Roman Emperor.

Despite continued admonition from the League and Britain, which feared a threat to its own empire, nothing was done to prevent or oppose Mussolini's impe-rialist strategies. The impotence of the democratic nations in confronting this inva-sion and annexation of a sovereign, peaceful country was the prelude to the Spanish Civil War and also the Second World War. It gave the fascists a green light to pursue their plans of world domination with impunity. However, for me, as young as I was, I could understand and empathise with those on the left who did recog-nise the significance of these events and valiantly tried to alert the wider public. Unfortunately the studied indifference of the ruling classes to the impending catas-trophe prevailed.

Nevertheless increasing numbers of ordinary working people realised that political turmoil was affecting mainland Europe and that Britain wouldn't be left unscathed. This was, of course, particularly so amongst the Jewish population in the East End, whose families' memories of persecution and pogroms were still very recent. Most working people also instinctively realised that the fascists were not on their side but represented the interests of a ruling elite and that their racialism and intolerance were opposed to the natural feelings of working class solidarity that characterised many communities at the time.

After the First World War, the influence of socialists and anarchists in the East End had declined significantly, and politically active Jews turned to the Labour or Communist Parties. Some immigrants sought to improve their condition through self-help, and friendly societies — many of which had been established in the 19th century — provided an important social framework as well as aid for members in times of hardship or ill-health. These organisations were elaborate, with their own regalia, rules and rituals. In London in 1901 there were 13 Jewish orders of friendly societies, with a total membership of almost 23,000. The Workers' Circle, a flourishing left-wing friendly society, was founded in 1909. It not only provided benefits for its members but also acted as an important educational, social and cultural club, organised from its headquarters in Circle House, Stepney. It drew its members from the left wing in the widest sense — trades union members, anarchists, communists, and socialists. The Circle's membership reached its highest levels in the late 1930s, when it became active in the fight against fascism.

The Salmon & Ball pub was at the junction of Bethnal Green Road and Cambridge Heath Road. Next door a building had been taken over by trade unionists and several progressive organisations. It began to be used regularly for political meetings and social gatherings. Outside there was a large open pavement space that became a de facto speakers' corner. Open-air meetings were held there on an almost daily basis, as well as in nearby Victoria Park Square that was a popular venue for larger gatherings.

Joe Morrison, I and a few others set up a local branch of the Labour Party's League of Youth, and we were very soon embroiled in the political fray. Our activities took place on the streets and in organising protests at fascist rallies, like the big ones Mosley staged at Olympia.

Regularly, but particularly on Monday mornings after the activities of the weekend, there would be a steady stream of anti-fascists appearing at Old Street Magistrates Court, to be fined or in some cases imprisoned for 'causing an affray' or a 'breach of the peace'. In those days the police and the legal profession tended to sympathise more with the fascists than with their opponents, and so it was mainly anti-fascists who were arrested. Many of those convicted made regular court appearances for the same or similar infringements. Joe Morrison was once standing under the railway bridge in Bethnal Green Road selling *Advance,* the League's paper when he was attacked by a group of young fascists from whom he ran, seeking shelter in the police station nearby, only to find himself charged with creating a disorder, as a consequence of which he lost his job.

Sometimes we would wander further a field to attend meetings. But, on occasions, if rarely, they would be held in the back room of the Nanking Restaurant in Denmark Street and would be followed by a group of comrades enjoying a Chinese meal together, over which the animated discussions would continue without let up. We never had much money and knew little or nothing about foreign foods, but we enjoyed the large servings. We were, though, disconcerted one day to see the proprietor eating a meal of lamb chops with chips!

The now infamous attempt by Mosley to march his blackshirts through the East End of London on Sunday 4th of October 1936 was intended to demonstrate their gathering strength, to show his followers that with the support of the establishment nowhere and nothing was sacrosanct, and to show the Jews and Leftists that they were at his mercy. The march, through the mostly Jewish occupied streets around Stepney in East London, was to be the culmination of a long period of sustained recruitment activity. They rallied at Tower Hill under the protection of a massed police force, whose Chief Constable was determined to ensure that they would march as planned. The Labour Party and the Jewish establishment advised everyone to stay out of the way; 'ignore it', was the watchword. Even the Communist Party, which had been the most active force opposing the fascists, appeared equivocal. Then, just one week before the event, following strong pressure from local members, the call went out from the Communist Party to defend the streets. Teams were dispatched to whitewash anti-fascist slogans on the walls, and meetings were held on practically every street corner. The *Daily Worker* proclaimed the call to defend the streets and not let the fascists through. It was a deliberate provocation they said and must be stopped. The rallying point was Gardeners' Corner, the junction of Whitechapel, Commercial Road and Commercial Street.

On the day, and as the fascists, under their leader Oswald Mosley, met in the shadow of the Tower of London, masses of local people and their supporters gathered in opposition. Gardeners' Corner and surrounding streets became a sea of heaving bodies. Extra police, both on foot and mounted, were drafted in to disperse and break them up. It developed into a mini-civil war − the police and fascists determined to march through and the local people determined to stop them. There were heavy clashes, but the police and fascists were beaten back, time and time again; barricades were thrown up and missiles thrown as tempers became inflamed. The turning point came when a tram driver refused to drive his vehicle

Police at the scene in Cable Street where Mosley's fascists where stopped by ordinary people determined to keep racism out of their neighbourhood - Sunday 4th October 1936.

onwards through the crowds and the resulting havoc led the Metropolitan Police to decide to by-pass the area and take the march on a different route. The fascists remained trapped on Tower Hill, surrounded and protected by a massive force of police, and frustrated by the action of thousands of Jews, trade unionists, socialists, communists and other ordinary people, determined to see justice defended. Despite all the efforts by the police, they were unable to guarantee the fascists' safety on that memorable day.

The anti-fascist organisers of the protest demonstration had managed to infiltrate the area of Tower Hill and became privy to police intentions. Additionally, they had taken precautions to cover those secondary streets that could have been used to let the march through. Nevertheless, it was inevitable that many unconfirmed rumours were flying about. One was that the march was to be diverted through Cable Street. I had, with a large group, already walked some six miles from Hackney Road to Gardeners and been involved in the general shoving and pushing that took place. When Cable Street was mentioned as being the new preferred route, I decided to go there, after all it was my old manor and I knew most of the people on that stretch of the road from Leman Street to Cannon Road, and my Grandmother still ran the bakery at number 86.

There was some confusion among the inhabitants of the Jewish 'colony', which would bear the immediate effect of the fascist incursion. This small section of the street from Back Church Lane to Cannon Street had to be traversed by the fascists

53

Front page report in the *Daily Herald* on the Cable Street battle.

if they were to progress any further. Many of the residents were elderly and, as I already mentioned, most retained vivid memories of the pogroms they and their parents had endured. Some were for shutting down to avoid trouble, but the majority were anxious to resist this fresh provocative incursion, and did come out onto the streets. The resistance took many forms: we 'borrowed' a flat bed truck, sufficiently long to close-off the street just before Fleming Street, and when news filtered through, we reinforced the barricade and more people came onto the streets.

My uncle Isaac from the fish and chip shop went immediately to his Pell Street stable and, fighting through the gathering crowd, tried to get his horse and cart out to use them to further hinder the fascists' progress. We were afraid he would attempt a gladiatorial battle all on his own.

When the first wave of mounted police arrived to clear the way, they were pelted from ground level with broken paving- and cobble-stones and from every window with missiles ranging from filled piss-pots to lumps of wood, rotten fruit and old bedding, all sorts of items rained down on them. There were hand-to-hand skirmishes and attempts to force the release of those arrested by the enemy.

Battle of Cable Street mural by Desmond Rochfort, Paul Butler, and Ray Walker in 1982/3 on the side of St. George's Hall, Cable Street, to commemorate the struggle against fascism.

Claims were made, and not without substance, that several police who were taken captive had surrendered voluntarily. Attempts to circumnavigate the resistance by means of mounted police riding in large numbers into nearby Wellclose Square via Fletcher Street and up through the sloping narrow North East Passage were beaten off. Then the timely arrival of a large number of dockworkers from the surrounding area reinforced and helped sustain the resistance. Recognising the potential of heavy casualties on both sides, and the overwhelming strength and determination of the anti-fascist resistance, the police reluctantly retreated. Throughout all this mayhem Mosley and his supporters could only strut back and forth impotently within the confines of Tower Hill, guarded by a massive phalanx of police.

The routing of Mosley's fascists and the 'Battle of Cable Street' have been well documented in a number of excellent books about that era and in an excellent programme in the BBC TV series, *Yesterday's Witness*, made by Stephen Peet. There is also the magnificent mural, commemorating the event, which still decorates an end of terrace wall on Cable Street.

On the Sunday following that great victory, there was a celebratory march along the route the fascists were prevented from marching. There I furthered an acquaintance with a very pretty young girl who I had often seen but never spoken to on the many occasions I'd traversed Bethnal Green Road or on my visits to the housing estate known as the Bandstand. Lily Weinberg and I started a courtship on that march, which blossomed into a real love affair that is still going strong today!

CHAPTER SIX
War in Spain and the start of a serious relationship

The Civil War in Spain, which broke out in 1936 was one of those momentous events that marked the seemingly inevitable rise of fascism in Europe and left an indelible mark on my generation. Defending the Spanish Republic became the rallying call for left-wing intellectuals and working class socialists throughout the world. We recognised that if Spain were defeated, then the rest of Europe would soon follow – and how right we were.

It was precipitated by the invasion of Spain from Morocco by General Franco and his fascist supporters in an attempt to topple the democratically elected Republican government. The British government, along with that of France and other democratic western European nations adopted a policy of 'non-intervention', which in reality meant that they gave no help to the Republican government while turning a blind eye to the massive support, in terms of weaponry and manpower, given to the fascist insurgents by Hitler's Germany and Mussolini's Italy.

Of course we protested and we marched but the most important contribution we made was to become involved in the Food for Spain movement. This was a countrywide exercise to collect and send vitally needed food to the besieged people of Spain. In our area, we hired a barrel organ and tramped the streets night after night knocking on doors to garner whatever we could. And we were proud of the contribution we made, however limited it was.

In connection with our work for Spain, my first real organising experience was arranging a moonlight ramble starting at The Teapot Café on Biggin Hill. It was also, I suppose, unconsciously my initiation into the holiday trade long before I had any inkling that I would, in later life, find my true vocation there. I priced the cost of a coach and the hire of the café in order to ensure that we would make enough profit, and advertised it in *Advance*, the League's paper, and in the *Daily Worker*.

The meeting place was Aldgate East Station. The evening was luckily warm and balmy and we soon had the first coach filled, and very shortly afterwards another one and still yet another one at the very last moment. Joe and Di Morrison, with two other friends, the Wormolds, went ahead and set up the sandwiches and tea which were included in the price. We also took with us an amateur jazz quartet. We made a lot of money for Spain through this initiative and at the same time had a great time doing so. I had to work hard on Lily's mother to allow Lily to go. It was her conviction, not without some reason in those days, that it wasn't right for a girl to be out all night with a boy, but at the very last moment she relented.

The opening of Victoria Park Lido in that year was an event of great importance to us as youngsters. My friends and Lily's, particularly Lily Orbach and René Schwartz, formed one of the many groups who during the hot summer months used this enormous pool. It had diving boards at different heights, a tearoom and a small shingle beach. Being a real innovation, it replaced Regent's Canal as our regular leisure 'pool'. The canal ran under the bridge at Mare Street, along Andrews Road and close to the junction with Hackney Road. Boys and men, never girls, would use it as an unofficial swimming pool. Unfortunately there were regular deaths among those choosing to dive from the bridge and then hitting the heavy mud at the bottom of the shallow waters, never to rise again, despite frantic searches, until the area had been dredged.

The approach to the Lido was via a vast open space that today is inevitably a car park. At that time it was a place for budding gymnasts who used the primitive and minimal equipment to practise their art, and attract the crowds that gathered to see muscular men swinging from ropes and rings attached to fixed poles. It was quite a walk to get there, but the park, with two different sections, separated by Grove Road with its trams lines, and covering almost 300 acres, was a fine example of the sort of urban initiatives undertaken in Victorian times during the booming expansion of industrial might and wealth.

It had a large lake with rowing boats for hire and for a penny you could take a passenger boat that traversed it. There were resplendent flower displays throughout the year and dozens of fountains. It was designed to provide North East London with 'a lung', and a place of escape from the claustrophobic streets and back-street tenements. The entrance-lodge, built in mock Elizabethan style, was designed by the architect, Sir James Pennethorne.

Victoria Park occupies lands that formerly belonged to the heretic-burning Bishop Bonner, and were known previously as 'Bonner's Fields'. There is still a Bonner Road joining Bishops Way, our entrance to the park. Close by was the Chest Hospital known to us as the place for consumptives – a common enough disease at the time among the under-nourished and over-worked people of the area.

My courtship with Lily turned out to be more than a short fling. She had left school at fourteen to become a clothing machinist. The two shillings and sixpence she received each week for working in the clothing factory was a vital contribution to her widowed mother's finances. But it was really too long a working day for her. Nevertheless we were able to be together most evenings. She was, like me, also politically aware and we both participated in the political activities on the streets. We also observed the events unfolding in mainland Europe with growing apprehension.

We met once a week after she finished work in Cleveland Street near Tottenham Court Road and would put two stools in the queue for the pit at the Holborn Empire. We'd ask someone to look after them for us and take turns keeping an eye on other people's stools while being entertained by the buskers, or we'd nip off to the nearby Lyons teashop and have the cheapest dish, egg on toast, before going back to join the queue. On special occasions we'd share a strawberry jam and cream waffle. We alternated this with the same procedure at the London Palladium; our seats cost sixpence. But we were able to experience performances by some of the greatest artistes of our time.

Max Miller was a very popular star whose jokes were so well known to the audience that they would finish them in tandem with him. My favourite music group, though, was Nat Gonella and his Georgians. I would walk many miles to hear them; it was my introduction to jazz.

Occasionally, if in the money, we would go to the Dominion Cinema in Tottenham Court Road and it was there, while watching the Movietone newsreel that we first learned of Chamberlain's return from Munich, waving his bit of paper and his weasel words, declaring, he had brought back 'peace in our time'. Well it wasn't much of a peace. Within weeks Hitler had invaded Czechoslovakia, and war for Britain loomed ever closer. We were shocked, and I still remember how we clung together tearfully, aware that his capitulation to Hitler had now made war inevitable.

My close friend, Joe Morrison, married his long time girl friend, Di Hallaman, while Lily and I continued our courtship. Just three months before war was declared Lily's family moved from their rooms in Old Nichol Street to larger premises on the top floor in Pentland House, a block of flats on a London County

Council estate at Stamford Hill in North London. Here there was a bathroom with a lavatory, but no hand washbasin − something I could never understand.

A year before I joined the army, the Labour League of Youth had been disbanded by the 1938 Labour Party Conference. Herbert Morrison explained at great length that our organisation had been taken over by the extreme left and had become an embarrassment to the leadership because we opposed their policies on a number of important issues. As I'd often worked alongside the Young Communist League in activities in support of the Spanish Republic and during the street resistance to fascism, it clearly became an option for me to join them, as a number of my fellow Labour Leaguers did, but I did neither. Why not? I think it was largely because I disliked bureaucracy and dishonesty. I encountered both in the Labour Party and I feared that the Communist Party would be little different, and what we now know, has proved me right. Although that was the political climate at the time, a number of us, for various reasons, didn't join any party, preferring to remain free to do things our own way. Yes, we had friends who were in either the Labour or Communist Party and with these we had avid discussions and arguments.

The disbanding of the Labour League of Youth meant that contact was lost with many friends. My political beliefs however did not change, and in many of them I was very close to the Young Communist League as well as being highly critical of the Labour Party − in particular its leadership − and I continued to participate in demonstrations and other activities. The League's paper, *Advance*, was never published again and many of those who had worked on it, like Ted Willis (later Lord Willis), the TV scriptwriter, Alec Bernstein (Alexander Baron) Doreen Williams, and Jim Mortimer, later General Secretary of the Labour Party, brought their talents to bear elsewhere, where they felt more able to express their political convictions.

In 1936, my grandfather, Alex Morris, died of cancer. My grandmother Ester carried on the business until finally, some months later, finding it too much for her, offered it to my father who, only too happy to run away from his own business, now in deep debt, accepted, and we did a 'moonlight flit'. For a while we lived with my grandmother until some months later she moved to Stamford Hill to live with Stella, who was now married, to leave us in charge of a rat and bug infested house. Despite all our financial problems in Hackney Road we had at least decent accommodation, including a bathroom and inside toilet, both still very much a rarity in those days. The change, though, was an awful blow for us. My mother now had the added burden of maintaining cleanliness in an unhygienic building and I, with rest of the family, had to use Betts Street Baths for my weekly ablutions.

The conditions in the Hackney bakery had been bad; most bakeries were in basements and all had coal-fired brick ovens. In Hackney there was a flight of stairs from the shop to what was, or should have been, the storeroom, but there was never much to store. From there you had to cross a tiny open yard and down a further four stone steps into the bakery. Above the bakery was the flour room from which flour was conveyed through an opening directly into the dough-making machine, through a hessian sack contraption.

As a boy I dreaded going into the bakery: the stairs were invariably caked with flour, and when wet, were extremely treacherous, and the light switch had a broken brass cover and was difficult to see in the dark. But my biggest fear was the myriad cockroaches or, as we called them, black beetles. I knew from experience that immediately I switched on the light the whole floor would seemingly start moving as they scurried in their hundreds to hide under the furniture and equipment. Often when I put up my hand gingerly to feel for the switch I would get an electric shock from the bare wires.

Cable Street bakery was also in the basement, but directly under the shop. Behind the bakery was the flour and storeroom which, as I remember when we first moved in, was well stocked. There was natural light from two windows that looked out onto a small yard in which there was a toilet and next to it a permanent 'Sukkah' where, during the Jewish holiday of Sukkas, we would sit with my grandparents and have our meal on returning from synagogue. The yard was open to the elements although covered with a trellis of vines from which hung bunches of grapes in the late summer months.

This was symbolic of the times when Jews lived in the open in roughly built huts and were entirely at the mercy of the elements. Since the Sukkas holiday was usually in early or mid-October there was often inclement weather. Traditionally, Sukkah comes at the end of the planting year and is called the Harvest Festival. After the harvest Jews are commanded to take the leftovers from the harvest, construct a Sukkah and dwell in it for seven days and rejoice. My grandfather insisted that on the first and last day of the holiday it was obligatory to sit and eat in the Sukkah despite any discomfort from the elements.

Living in Cable Street opened up new possibilities for my father. The spielers were closer, the gambling made easier and some of the characters he met there he found attractive. One in particular was a recognised burglar, but he was no Bill Sykes. He was very tall, handsome and well dressed in the most expensive suits, always a charmer and known as Slim. He was not one of the 'heavies'; everyone knew his trade, and my father more than once expressed the opinion that I should be more like Slim — maybe a successful 'gunoff' (i.e. a thief), and not as he saw me: one of life's losers, with my 'squeamish morality', unwilling to risk stepping outside legal boundaries.

I always find myself taking the high moral ground whenever I discuss, or are questioned about, my father and his siblings. With the exception of the youngest, uncle Woolfie, the other three were gamblers to the point of self-destruction. All of them were first class craftsmen and if, instead of devoting their lives to gambling, they had worked towards the success of their businesses, if they had combined their skills and knowledge, they could have created, even if not an empire, then at least a substantial well-organised bakery business.

Grodginzki (perhaps the most famous of the Jewish bakeries) started at about the same time, as a small family business, and moved on to higher things, as did Kossof. Both were successful family concerns. I know there was greater potential initiative from both my father and my uncle Ruby, than in most of the other East End bakers. It was uncle Ruby who introduced American pink and white coconut ice, produced in slabs and made fresh each day. My father's fruitcake was superior to any I have ever eaten. He sold doughnuts in the hundreds daily, but it all went into 'drosh'.

He was forever coming up with 'get rich quick' ideas. For instance, my mother, as did a lot of Jewish women of her time, made her own lockshen (vermicelli). It was made with eggs and I can still remember how tasty it was. She made it in the kitchen. She would roll out the fresh dough in an ever-widening circle until it became almost translucent, then hang it up to dry. After gauging the correct time, she would cut the dough through the centre making two half moons, then roll them from the top into a long string from which she cut thin slices from one end.

My father suddenly decided that this could be a 'good seller' and fully expected my mother to produce mountains of vermicelli in addition to all the other tasks she had. It was shortly afterwards that Rakusens produced a similar, but not nearly so good, commercial version of her lokshen.

It was Ruby's youngest son, Harvey, who showed how it could and should be done. With the assistance of his wife Dianne they built up a chain of bakery shops and a factory to supply them out of a converted Sainsbury building in Hatch End. The only one of the Morrisses still in the trade is Harvey's son Simon who has a flourishing business in Ruislip High Street in Middlesex. Simon's bakery is the archetypal one-man business of which, as I recall from my youth, there were so many, and where hard work and endeavour was often successful.

At the top of Christian Street, near the junction with Commercial Street there was a narrow passage that issued into a small bakery where the sole product on sale was bagels. It was the domain of two brothers, apparently twins. Bagels were

a part of the staple diet in Jewish families and there is the eternal tale of two elderly ladies who sold them from hessian sacks each on opposite sides of the
entrance to the original Blooms' on the corner of Old Montague Street and Brick
Lane. It didn't matter from which one you purchased your bagels you would be
showered with vehement curses from the other. It was so much part of the process
that if on occasion it failed to materialise, you were surprised and curious enough
to ask why. These two harridans purchased their product from this small bagel
bakery in Christian Street and there is no doubt that they were selling originals,
not like those poor mass-produced imitations on sale in supermarkets these days.
I was known to the bagel bakers even from a very young age and I would visit
them quite often.

Making bagels is so different from the type of baking that my family were
involved in. The dough is made from stronger flour producing a tighter and less
manipulable dough. There was a hand pull machine which cut the large, weighed
pieces into the required size of the bagel and it was then rolled by hand, both
ends joined to make a circle. The soft bagels were then boiled in water.

The oven was of red brick and coal-fired from the side. When the bagels had
been boiled sufficiently, they were placed on a 'peel', a tapered flat board some 15
by 25 inches square, to which was attached a short pole. The 'peel' was 'floured'
because the bagels, being moist, there was always the problem of them sticking
to the board. It still happened, and to overcome this the brothers each had a
length of thin but strong string around their neck, and once the peel was loaded,
they would quickly and deftly sweep the string between the bagel and the board
then swiftly place the batch in the oven. Unhygienic it probably was, but very effective and, they claimed, it enhanced the flavour.

In Fieldgate Street, a small street that ran parallel with Whitechapel Road, and
at the rear of the old Rivoli Cinema (now a mosque) there was a small bakery that
was also run by twin brothers. They were niche bakers, their speciality being
'Lubbons', large black loaves weighing probably seven to ten pounds each which
were sold to grocery shops where they would be retailed in portions. This was an
Eastern European speciality bread which instead of using yeast for fermentation,
used dough from the previous night's bake (so-called sour-dough baking).

The only place I have tasted anything like it is at the Hungarian restaurant,
Gay Hussar, in Soho where we hold our Anjou Luncheon Club events. These
brothers were weightlifting and wrestling fanatics and their bodies epitomised their
dedication. Neither was more than about five feet in height, but strongly built, they
were almost the original five by fives. There were times when I called in on them,
when having finished their night's work, they would spend their free time lifting
weights or having a tussle!

CHAPTER SEVEN
From conscription to marriage

C hamberlain returned to Britain in 1938 after signing the Munich
Agreement at his infamous meeting with Hitler, waving his piece of
paper like a winning lottery ticket, avowing it guaranteed 'peace in our
time', but this hardly assuaged our misgivings. Our greatest fears were
soon realised as Hitler proceeded to march into little Czechoslovakia,
and, shortly thereafter, Poland, making a European-wide war inevitable.
On the morning that Britain declared war on Germany, and the first
sirens were heard wailing outside, my father came dashing into the room
where I was listening to the news and shouted that it was all my fault. It
was my support for the Soviet Union and Russian treachery in invading
Poland that was the cause of it all. Yelling hysterically, he struck me a
hard blow across the face. This came as a terrible shock, despite years
of having expected it, and his fierce attack was also devastating psychologically. It was not the moment to try and argue with him rationally, and
I decided not to react, but leave him time for reflection. My only thought
was that these events were simply yet another excuse for him to vent his
anger and frustration on me. I left the house and walked the streets, saddened and reflective, mulling over thoughts of those past few years during which I'd become politically involved and active.

I recalled the perfidious behaviour of the Chamberlain government,
reneging on the trilateral agreement with France and Russia to aid
Czechoslovakia in the event of an invasion by Hitler. The close affinity
of the government and its ruling class with Hitler and his philosophy was

Lily and I on a Young Communist League day trip to the Isle of Wight, 1938.

hardly a secret. Hitler's virulent anti-Bolshevism and even his anti-Semitism were welcomed in ruling circles — he was seen as a bulwark against
the expansion of communism.

When Moscow called for urgent talks to formulate a common
response to the Nazi threat, the government despatched William Strange,
a middle-ranking civil servant in the Foreign Office, to Moscow, to discuss an issue that should have been the task of the Foreign Secretary.
To add insult to injury, despite the urgency of the matter, they sent him
by sea and rail, clearly indicating the level of priority they attached to his
mission. It was true, of course, that, although I was not a member of the
Communist Party, I had supported the Soviets to the hilt. I truly believed
that their's was the only real alternative to a system I found abhorrent.
Nevertheless I was forced to question my own motivation and action,
which I did, and found little difficulty in justifying all I had done.

Although war had been declared, no military action took place or was immediately planned. Nevertheless, young men were being called up for military service, and I was among the second wave of conscripted militia to be called. I reported to Whipps Cross Hospital for a medical. Passed fit, I joined the Duke of Wellington Regiment at Seaton Barracks, Crownhill, on the outskirts of Plymouth on the 1st December 1939.

On arrival at the barracks, I was a bit taken aback, but realised I should have guessed − a large section of my platoon came from Bethnal Green and among them were many followers of Britain's home-grown fascist leader, Oswald Mosley. I was the only Jew. George Day was the most prominent of these Mosleyites. His brother was Albie Day, a fine young boxer, who was seduced by the fascists and paraded as a paragon of Aryan youth. Every time he fought there would be conflict among the audience, as his fascist supporters provocatively agitated on his behalf and exaggerated his prowess. The reason he became such a symbol for the fascists was clear: the then British champion at his weight was a Jewish fighter called Harry Mizler, a fishmonger from Hessell Street Market in Stepney. He had fought his way up from modest beginnings as an amateur boxer with the Oxford and St. George Jewish Youth Club. They clamoured for a match between the two of them and eventually succeeded. The two met at the Devonshire Hall in Brenthouse Road, off Mare Street in Hackney, and Day was taught a painful lesson. He was so severely beaten that he never fought again; the Mosleyites quickly dropped their pet icon.

The first weeks of training in the army were traumatic, but it was not the physical tasks − they were hardly demanding. What was outrageous was route marching to the strains of the Nazi youth anthem: the Horst Wessell song, which Day and his followers persisted in whistling. (This song commemorated the death of a young Nazi, supposedly killed by communists, but who had in fact been a pimp and was killed in a pub brawl). I protested about this to senior NCOs, but evinced the retort: 'Stop your moaning − it's a nice tune'. Pleasant times during these months of training were few and far between, but one bucolic image I still retain, is of sitting on a hill overlooking the River Tamar, surrounded by a sea of yellow daffodils. It was true, I'd seen daffodils in Victoria Park, but never such a magnificent and overpowering sight as this one.

There were occasional visits to Plymouth and trips across the river by the antiquated chain ferry into St. Austel, to the firing range, but otherwise we were largely confined to barracks. Eventually the animosities with many of my 'enemies' eased. We found, probably because of our

Rookies together – I am third from left – Seaton barrcks near Plymouth in 1940.

similar working class backgrounds, that we had more things in common than divided us. Many of us supported Clapton Orient F.C. and commiserated with each other accordingly! Although we had often opposed each other in school football teams, and despite political differences, we did have mutual acquaintances, particularly among the boxing fraternity. Although most fighters were indifferent to politics, one great friend and someone with a strong political commitment was Harry Davis who on several occasions fought Johnny Cunningham for the Southern area light middleweight title. These bouts were sometimes won and sometimes lost – there were regular contests between the two at the local York Hall baths.

Boxing was a sport I was very interested in and I enjoyed being part of the boxing scene. In those days, before football became virtually the only sport talked about, boxing, particularly in working class areas, claimed a strong following. Whenever I could, I went to the Bethnal Green Men's Institute gym, which was frequented by many amateur and professional fighters, as well as numbers of overseas all-in wrestlers.

Through no fault of my own, I eventually found myself attached to the Arthur Danahar stable, sparring the odd few rounds. Danahar was preparing to defend his title in a fight with Eric Kid Boon from Chatteris in Cambridgeshire. It was, I believe the very first fight to be televised in Britain. Danahar lost because his father, who was his trainer, insisted he fight at a weight he had outgrown, and had starved him accordingly! This, plus a savage mauling I once witnessed between Arthur's elder brother and another boxer, Gardner, who was well past his prime, at York Hall baths, was one of several reasons that eventually dissuaded me from becoming more deeply involved, despite encouragement to do so from a number of quarters.

I fully expected to have opportunities for playing serious soccer while in the army, but this was not immediately possible. In my first days at Seaton, I was among those chosen from my platoon to attend a Rugby practice. A captain, who had us on parade, inspected us, and according to his own criteria, decided who would make good Rugby players, and I was one. From where I came from, Rugby was a toff's game. I did not have a clue what it was about and had little interest in finding out. Nevertheless I was chosen for the second row in the pack, which I later learned meant that I was in the thick of the shoving and heaving most of the time. It was head down and lock in with a bunch of other sweaty blokes to hold on to, and push, bloody well push!

I played eleven games for an Army Western Division team which was not too much of a problem when the opposing teams were amateurs from other services, but when I found myself pitted against players in senior league teams like Plymouth Albion, with experienced rugger players of international standard, it became a brutal one-sided battle. Finally having been sat upon by a mountain of burly Plymouth policeman, and having one ear almost torn from its moorings, one leg bloodied by skid marks from boot studs, plus a black eye, I decided to call it a day and returned to the working man's sport.

I came home on my first leave of the year for four days, and in that short break Lily and I agreed to get engaged. When I mentioned our intention to my mother, all hell broke loose, and I returned to barracks, bowed and disconsolate. I mulled it over and decided that if I was going to end up quarrelling over every move I made in life, then why should I hang about. Since Lily and I had decided to get married, why not do it? So with Lily's agreement I wrote and asked my mother to make the arrangements. Only after pressure from my grandmother Esther, did she agree, and we were duly married by the Cantors Myerovitch and Kusevitsky at the Duke's Place synagogue in the City of London − the flagship of British synagogues.

My mother was so grievously opposed to our nuptial troth that she decided to walk to the synagogue through the snow in her galoshes and had dressed as if going to my funeral rather than my wedding!

There was no reception − Lily's mother could not afford to pay for one, and my parents wouldn't, no doubt because this would be seen as condoning my misalliance. We held a small party in Lily's flat and a great time was had by all except my own family − not one of them was there.

CHAPTER EIGHT

I join the Green Howards and am sent to France

The leave for me to get married lasted three very short days. Then two months after I returned to barracks, and having completed the course, I was sent to Middlesbrough to join a territorial battalion of the Green Howards. There was a large number in this intake all of whom had been in the same barracks as me, but not necessarily in the same regiment. We were billeted at the local drill hall and integrated into what had been a small unit, with seemingly more officers than men. The locals were older than us and had greater cohesion by the mere fact that they were local. However, I soon had reason to doubt their experience and their abilities.

There were also contingents from other regiments, all rookies, but it soon became apparent that there was a shortage of lower-rank officers and NCOs. Apparently it was not possible to find men for these ranks outside, consequently there were immediate promotions. All officers and NCOs were bumped up a rank, irrespective of ability or experience. Other rankers from among the Territorials were made NCOs and as this took place while we were on parade many of us were dumbfounded. That shambles was transformed into the Sixth Battalion, the Green Howards.

In early March, and with no special leave granted, we suddenly found ourselves on the way to France. We landed at Le Havre and moved on to a small village called Yvetote, to await further orders. I was billeted on a local farm, and having spent most of my life in a bustling city, this was a new experience for me. There was a large brick-built oval pit into which hay and other plant matter were tipped. It clearly attracted myriad insects, and dense flocks of swallows constantly circumnavigated the parameters set by the brickwork of this contraption. With little else to do, I read a book, but with one eye fixed on this avian spectacle. I stayed at the farm for a short time, before we moved to Sedan as a support battalion to defend the 'impregnable' Maginot Line. However, I had to drive twice to the nearby town of Lille. Lille was the major city in the centre of a large industrial and commercial landscape. It had experienced a turbulent past, having been in the hands of the French, the Austrians and, long before that, even been occupied by Spain. It was badly damaged during the First World War and suffered once again during the Second.

Our visits were limited as to where we were allowed to go; it was a bleak and forbidding place. Because I could drive, I was attached to the transport pool, which made things easier when we needed a motor for getting about, and this fact also allowed us to see other nearby cities, like Amiens and Arras. I drove cars and Bedford 5 cwt trucks, also coaches and heavy goods vehicles that had been commandeered for army use. In between I participated in the minimal training we were given, but most of my time was taken up with an intensified spit, polish and drill that I grew to accept as one of the essential, if mind-numbingly boring, chores of men about to be transformed into killing machines.

There was great confidence in the impregnability of the Maginot Line, which had taken nine years to build, and was intended to deter any planned German incursion. Unfortunately, it had never been tested, and its supposed impenetrability proved to be wishful thinking. The Nazis didn't bother trying to smash through it, they simply went around it, out-flanking and exposing us to the serious danger of being trapped behind their rapidly advancing panzer divisions, that spearheaded the attack and ploughed relentlessly forward.

Near to where we were based was a battalion of the Durham Light Infantry, and we were all part of the 50th Division of the 8th Army. We had been told that Sedan was the pivotal defensive position for supporting the French army defending the Maginot Line. When all hell broke loose around the 11th May 1940, and the Nazis thrust unremittingly forward, we were immediately thrown onto the defensive and were ill-prepared for their onslaught.

I am not a military expert, despite my almost seven years' soldiering experience during the war, and am reluctant to be critical, but I was appalled by our lack of preparation and of clear strategy. We lacked appropriate weaponry and, even more, we lacked proper leadership; the

In February 1940 Lily and I tie the knot.

majority of us were inexperienced, but we became the vanguard given the task of blocking the Nazi advance.

Sometime later we learned that we were to be relieved by the Welsh Guards, but meanwhile we were being bombed by Nazi planes and strafed by their machine guns. We had no cover or camouflage, so were sitting ducks for them. Our instructions were to stop the motorcyclists with their sidecars but to ignore the waves of tanks. The motorcyclists were heavily armed with machine guns and grenades. They drove forward quickly and easily even across difficult terrain. They knew exactly where they were headed and their manoeuvrability was exceptional. We were reduced to staying put and, like hypnotised rabbits, were mesmerised as these swarming waves of soldiers swept past us. We were ensconced in ditches or narrow, hastily dug, trenches and armed only with Lee Enfield rifles and insufficient ammunition.

Comrades of mine were soon lying dead or severely injured beside me, but I could do little to help. We had no back-up until several days of intense fighting had taken place. My 21st birthday was spent crouched deep in a trench, where I was congratulated by a ragged mob of comrades, but with not a drop of alcohol between us to celebrate the occasion.

At one time, during a lull, we sheltered in a disused farm building, to hide from the planes zooming over us. Out of sheer frustration, we set up makeshift tripods on which we balanced machine guns that had been discarded by the roadside and started firing. We had never been trained to use them, and just shot wildly into the void. We couldn't record hitting anything, but it helped us feel better by offering some show of resistance.

As usual in such situations, with no hard facts or information to go on, rumours flourished. One of the most persistent was that we were to be the supporting regiment for a counter-attack led by our tanks, although we were unaware any existed. An effort was to be made, according to the rumour, to split off the fast moving German tanks from their supporting infantry. In the end we gathered that the Durham Light Infantry had been used to do this, because they were faster, but they suffered heavy losses in the exercise.

Eventually, a message trickled through, telling us we were to retreat to Dunkirk and to get there as best we could. There were three trucks nearby and everyone who was able, scrambled aboard. I drove the lead truck, packed solidly, followed by the other vehicles. It was a hazardous journey, made even more so by the fact that we weren't keen to waste any time.

CHAPTER NINE
Retreat from Dunkirk

The roads were clogged with refugee families, together with their chattels and animals, blocking our route at every juncture. At the roadside and in the fields alongside, the corpses of horses, cattle and human beings lay rotting. Overturned and abandoned vehicles had been dumped where they were and often blocked our path and had to be removed before we could continue. All the time, during our trek, Nazi aircraft kept up their bombardment of the roads and fields around us. Our frustration and impotence in the face of this debacle took a devastating psychological toll on all of us. And, we were avowedly military men and could be expected to cope with such situations in times of war. The civilian families, with children and babes in arms, their sole possessions carried in bags and cases, were completely at the mercy of the full might of the Nazi war machine − it was obscene. We felt helpless, for what these civilians were facing was ten times worse than what we had to face, and too awful to contemplate.

We reached a fork in the road, but there were no signposts and I had to guess which route to take. The driver immediately behind took the alternative road, but the third followed me. After the war was over, I met some of those who had taken the other route and was told they had been captured almost immediately by the Germans. So once again fate had been kind to me.

In all the time of our retreat we had not set eyes on a single officer and hardly a senior NCO. But just as we arrived a few miles from the Albert Canal, we met a small group of soldiers led by a Captain Hancock.

He was a rotund, fussy little man for whom nobody had any time, but it was he who brought us together and imposed some cohesion and collectivity on our movements.

Later that evening another small group met up with us, and among them was an adjutant who was extremely concerned to ensure the safe passage for a nearby truck. I later learned that this vehicle contained what had been saved from the officers' mess bar! I was instructed to drive it with him seated next to me, on what I thought was to be a reconnaissance trip, but which turned out to be my last leg as a driver.

He had no doubt hoped that he could salvage the valuable contents of the truck, however, when we reached the canal, we found it ablaze. Fire was everywhere — most buildings were alight, as were the bridges, far into the distance; vehicles and burning debris were collapsing into the canal. As we were still being subject to steady bombardment from the air, he decided to call it a day and desert our valuable booty.

The last order he gave me was to smash up the truck and destroy its contents so that the 'Jerries' wouldn't get hold of it. He disappeared very quickly and was so eager to get away that he took my greatcoat and helmet. I didn't realise this until I'd finished destroying the engine and smashing the cases of drink. I was obliged to take his 'warm' and helmet, which I wore till I reached Blighty. I heard no more of Major Leslie Petch — that was my compatriot's name — until years later, when I saw his name as chief steward at a number of northern racecourses. He had become a leading member of the Northern England Society.

After ensuring that the truck and its cargo were thoroughly unusable, I found I was completely on my own. I continued on foot, heading for the Albert Canal which had to be crossed before I could reach the coast. The Germans were bombing the bridges that straddled this wide stretch of water, and as I joined others heading in the same direction I found that no one knew if there was a single bridge left that was still crossable.

Reaching a higher vantage point on the canal bank, I could see that the whole area, including sections of the canal itself, was aflame. Men and officers were wandering around aimlessly, either alone or in small groups. Some were inebriated already, others were on their way to intoxication, most appeared to be suffering from shock, exhaustion and disorientation.

I eventually managed to get across the water over one of the few remaining bridges which even then was under heavy fire. I then headed westwards along the road littered with abandoned army trucks — French ones in the main, but some British. I then realised that the trucks had been, and still were in some cases, the source of the abundant liquor supply. I was myself gasping for a drink, but not alcohol, and I had hardly eaten for several days. I begged a French soldier, who was busily rummaging through a vehicle, for 'un peu de l'eau', but was presented with a bottle of a fizzy drink that turned out to be genuine champagne – the first time in my life I'd savoured it. I recalled the fierce battle that had taken place on my 21st birthday and the lack of a celebratory drink. Sitting helplessly there in a makeshift trench on that day, this champagne would have been a godsend, but now after what I'd seen happening around me, I didn't feel like a belated celebration, and one mess tin of the stuff was enough, before I staggered on.

Getting closer to the beaches, I passed sections of the 4th Battalion of the Welsh Guards who were dug in positions as the final rearguard. Each time I asked for information, the soldier recognising the crown on my helmet and the epaulettes on the British warm I was wearing, would salute me before speaking. From my conversations, I learned that Dunkirk was now ablaze and that the best bet was to head for Gravelines or Bray Dunes, north of that fated city. It was the latter that I finally reached, to find that it was exactly as its name implied: a broad, windswept desert like beach with high dunes on its landward edge.

Looking back up the coast, the skeleton of what had been Dunkirk was just visible through the flames and the black billowing smoke. And still the Luftwaffe was releasing its full complement of bombs on what was left of the city. At the same time the German fighter aircraft, mainly Messerschmitts, strafed us incessantly.

Many servicemen had dug simple holes in the dunes, where they sheltered, suffering as they were from fatigue and exhaustion. For a few moments I thought I would do the same, as I hadn't slept for days, but in my search for somewhere suitable I came across several dead bodies with bullet and shrapnel wounds. I swore this was not going to be my fate.

On the beach itself thousands of men were scattered willy-nilly, waiting for rescue. From the variety of uniforms, I could see they were men from a number of regiments, and all revealed the harrowing stress of their recent experiences.

At one end of the long beach a ship was stranded in low water – it had suffered a direct hit. I was told it was an Isle of Man steamer, which in peace time normally ferried people from Liverpool to Douglas on the Isle of Man. As it had suffered a direct hit immediately following embarkation, there had been heavy casualties.

After Dunkirk, in 1941 I was posted to the Wiltshire Regiment.

Continuing to defy the horrific dangers, smaller boats persisted in edging towards the beach; others were already leaving, heavily laden with a motley cargo of servicemen. In the distance larger vessels, seemingly anchored, were either waiting to load or were already taking fleeing troops on board, as I could make out sailors assisting those who had made it. It was a surreal scene: the warm colours of the late evening sunshine turning the whole seascape a deep crimson and for the occasional moment there would be a comparative silence, and I felt it was all like a still from a film.

With a single exception, it was total chaos: all along the beach men lay, each covered only with a blanket or greatcoat; there was an overwhelming air of desperate despondency. A large number of men were in the water, wading, swimming or paddling in their effort to reach a vessel – their only chance to get home safely. The one exception was a line of signalmen under the command of a senior officer who had posted guards around the straggling group of men, preventing intruders joining the queue. He was directing small craft to come to him, attempting to hog whatever was available and having some success.

In the end, I did find shelter in the dunes for a few hours during the darkness. At daybreak, I decided to take my chance in the water and attempt to reach a boat. I retained my rifle which I'd carried all this way, took off my boots, tied the laces together, and hung them round my neck. In I went, walking through the shallow water until I was unable to go any further and then, slowly to retain what energy I still had, I ditched the rifle and swam some considerable distance until I was eventually pulled aboard a small vessel. In its civilian role this boat normally carried East Londoners on holiday trips around the coast near Southend. I was then transferred from this boat to HMS Codrington, where I was given a very welcome hot drink, after which I fell into a deep sleep until we reached Dover. I later learned that this ship was subsequently hit by German bombers while undergoing repairs and sunk.

We were loaded on to waiting trains at the dockside and I dozed fitfully on the journey, until I was suddenly woken by bedlam. The train had arrived at Euston Station and the boys couldn't believe their luck until it was realised that all the doors had been locked and the only way we could have got out, would have been to scramble through the windows. But before we were able to do that, the train immediately steamed out of the station again. That was Saturday 2nd June 1940. You can imagine how disgruntled we all were. After what seemed another endless journey we arrived at the chemical warfare base at Winterbourne, near Salisbury (which later became the notorious Porton Down biological research station). At least here we were given our first proper sit-down meal after what seemed like an eternity.

The next morning I phoned Lily to let her know I was safe. I had breakfast and walked to the village. It was a glorious morning and I lay on the grass listening to music that came seemingly from nowhere. On the village green a cricket match was in progress. This was another world of normality and calm; my recent experiences seemed never to have happened — perhaps they had been just a nightmare, I thought. I fell asleep to the uneven rhythm of the dull thud of leather ball on bat and the strains of Greensleeves from an open window in one of the village houses.

A very good friend of mine, Len Lermer, from the days when I first arrived in Hackney Road, kindly offered to drive Lily out to see me one Sunday. It was a great idea, except that both my mother and father insisted on coming too! This meant that Lily and I had very little time on our own, so she agreed to come again on her own the Sunday following. However, on that morning, and without notice, we were moved to Launceston in Cornwall, but Lily was already on the train on her way to meet me.

I was desperate to let her know that I hadn't just deserted her, so I asked a WVS woman who was dishing out tea if she would look out for her and explain why I wasn't there. I gave her the only photograph I had, so that she would recognise Lily. She kept her promise, met Lily and saw her back on to the London train. It was a bitter disappointment for both of us — it seemed we were never destined to consummate our marriage, which for various reasons we'd not been able to do on our honeymoon. This wasn't the way either of us had envisaged our first months of marriage.

In Cornwall, the task of rebuilding the battalion was undertaken. Then, after a short stay there, we were moved to Hampshire to bolster the coastal defences. First we had an intake of 300 men from the Cameron Highlanders, then there was the re-establishment of discipline and training. Our initial base was in the grounds of a large estate at Hinton Admiral. We were living under canvas and were plagued by a flock of peacocks in the grounds. The birds produce the most appallingly loud and raucous calls. Several patrols were formed in an attempt to eliminate the birds but with little success.

Our leisure time was spent in the Cat and Fiddle, just beyond the gates of the estate. It was a typical country inn, frequented by the locals people with whom we developed friendly relations. In addition to the beer, there were darts, shove ha'penny and skittles. Among members of the battalion, too, we had developed a stronger feeling of comradeship.

After our arrival on the estate, we were required to collect requisitioned motor cycles from Godfrey's motor cycle store in Southampton which sold new and second-hand bikes of all descriptions. Very few of us knew how to handle a bike, but that didn't deter our superiors from giving us a few tips and sending us on our way. I never regretted that I learned to ride a Harley Davidson there, and continued to use one for some time. Later I was deputed to drive a truck to Croydon to collect motorbikes from Godfrey's, then on to their store at Stamford Hill, which was fortuitously no more than half a mile from where Lily was living and which was to become my home for many years after the war ended.

Of course Lily was there to meet me after I made a brief phone call. I was able to steal a short time with her before driving on to Albany Road Barracks at Regents Park, where we were promptly confined to barracks. Well what would you do in such a circumstance? We six Londoners in the party simply went AWOL and returned the next morning.

The Nazi bombardment of London had started early in September and continued unabated for many months. Even when it lessened, there was still the constant threat. Lily, with her mother, continued to live in their new top floor flat. She worked in a factory making sleeping bags and mattresses for the government. At the beginning of each evening she and her mother went down into the makeshift and cramped shelters that had been provided by the authorities.

The bombing intensified and there were not enough shelters for all the people, so a big campaign erupted to force the government to open up the tube stations as night shelters. This was resisted for a time, but local action, often by left-wing activists, forced the government to relent. Each evening they would gather their parcels of bedding, food and drink and make their way to Holborn station where eventually they had a regular section of the platform to themselves. They continued to do this until the air raids abated. All through those months they and thousands of other Londoners did the same, showing great strength, bravery and resilience. Through all the victories and the defeats associated with the war years their determination and camaraderie was outstanding. In comparison, the role I was obliged to play in the following years seemed very inadequate.

Some eighteen months after my return from France and having experienced several postponed embarkation dates, we were moved to Marston Hall in Frome, Somerset. After being inspected by Field Marshal Montgomery, we knew that this time it was for real. Rumour had it that we were to be sent somewhere in the North African desert.

The routine for the morning of our leaving meant a medical inspection at 5.30 am followed by breakfast and pay parade. On pay parade my name was called, but as I went to the table there was another Lance Corporal A. Morris who had answered the call — he was one of the Scottish lads. The officer asked our numbers and said to me: 'not you, fall out'. I was utterly confused, and only later did I discover that I couldn't go, as the medical officer had declared that my hearing had been damaged, by the events in Flanders before my evacuation from France, and had left me with a perforated eardrum. I was downgraded. I recalled that in the early confrontations at that time I had suffered intolerable headaches and had had a perpetual discharge from my ear. I had paid it little attention, attributing it to the noise and the fear factor.

It was a strange feeling − I had been with my platoon for almost two years and with a few comrades even longer. I'd made many friends and probably for the first time in my service life, felt comfortable in the army. There was also a feeling of pride in the way we had become a band of efficient warriors.

I stayed on in Frome until I was posted to Catterick Barracks, near Richmond in Yorkshire. After one week there I was posted-on to the Wiltshire Regiment at Bulford Camp on Salisbury Plain where I was put in charge of a small platoon of fellow rejects and walking wounded. Again we were under canvas with absolutely nothing to do. We became the forgotten men. No other NCO, but me, and no officers to assist or bully us − it should have been a layabout's paradise, but I found life there dreary and aimless.

After a week of pointless, unfocussed activity, I suggested that we organise ourselves and do some sport, so we began playing five-a-side football and makeshift cricket. In the evenings we gathered in the largest tent and talked. I discovered that we had a former Midlands ABA boxing champion, two miners, an accountant, among others who had a variety of jobs and hobbies in civvy street. With their agreement I set up a programme to keep us occupied and amused. Each of us was to talk on any subject we wished. Most spoke about their job, one lectured us on racing pigeons, the boxer told of his rise to, and fall from, fame, the miners told us about their work underground and of life in a mining village. We were shocked to hear about their poverty, despite their doing one of the most vital, dirty and demanding jobs in the country − mining coal for all of us. We heard first hand the difficulty they had in adjusting to smoking real tobacco instead of dried tea leaves which was all they could normally afford.

I opened discussions about the war and the political context, only to discover an abysmal lack of knowledge about how the system worked. Another Jewish chap, a tailor named Hillman who was well into his forties, was utterly bemused by his surroundings. He was still wondering how he had been called up into the armed forces at all. He introduced us to Einstein's theory of relativity and did it remarkably well, using very simple illustrations.

This 'inactivity' was another of those very enlightening periods of my life. For years I had been advocating the lot of the underdog and discussing political theory, because I'd seen much poverty and suffering in the East End, mainly as a result of unemployment as well as bigotry. In those few weeks I learned once again how people are able to cope in adversity, despite disabilities and disappointments.

CHAPTER TEN
My new roles - teacher of motor mechanics and that of father

I was at Bulford camp for about five weeks, before I was again posted, this time as a driving and motorcycling instructor to 164OCTU, which I soon learned stood for: Officer Cadet Training Unit, on the Isle of Man. My main duties were to teach cadets how to drive, to understand the workings of a motor vehicle and be able to carry out minor repairs. Today's generation, looking back to that period, would find it hard to believe that very few people then could drive, let alone own a car or motorcycle.

The driving and motorcycling was the reasonably easy bit to teach. In the main, it involved taking my cadets around the famous TT circuit. Now that I was quite proficient at handling a motorcycle, I tackled the more difficult sections at high speeds, and this really got my adrenalin flowing.

I found giving lectures a bit difficult to begin with, but after a while became more comfortable with my subject. The cadets were, in the main, university and grammar school-educated men, some much older and far more experienced than me. In my audience there would invariably be someone with an engineering or electronics degree, or a motor mechanic with years of experience and I learned quickly to use them when difficulties of interpretation or analysis arose, which, due to my limited knowledge and vocabulary, it did on occasions.

Sometimes the debates we had on all sorts of subjects became quite intense. I gradually came to a better understanding and appreciation of the differences in attitude and perspective reflected by these future 'leaders of men'. My past experience had made me extremely cynical and distrustful of the 'toffs', but it was rewarding to encounter people of very different backgrounds and education from my own.

I was also used as driver by the senior officers, and in doing this I learned much of the history of the unit. The officer commanding was a Colonel Bull, and apparently he had been Principal of Imperial College, and his unit had been structured on the same basis as that institute, with most officers drawn from the lecturers. There were also other senior officers who were war veterans with real battle experience. But how antiquated their views were, I soon gathered by listening to their conversations. They seemed to be still fighting the 'Khyber Pass' battles and other old colonial wars, often expressing anti-Semitic, racist and wildly reactionary views. It required a great deal of restraint on my part to remain silent when driving three high ranking officers and hearing them speak disparagingly of Jews, blacks and the local Manx people. Changes did come about though when a new CO, Major Niven, took over and brought in a different breed of officer.

Later I was sent to the Ford motor works at Dagenham for a two-week course on Bren Gun Carriers. I had been told that they had been used in action when I was in France, although we saw none in our battalion, or if there were, I cannot recall any. I returned to the Isle of Man as the specialist instructor on Bren Gun Carriers which were due to arrive shortly and become an important part of training. Fords were the main manufacturers although they were soon to be produced in great numbers also in Australia, Canada, New Zealand and even the USA, where they were known as T16s; they later became known as Universal Carriers. They were envisaged as fast, lightly armoured track vehicles (Bren Gun) with a crew of from two to four. They had a V8 water-cooled engine and only 12mm armoured plating. It was really just a petrol engine mounted in the middle of the chassis, with a gate gearbox. Because it was fully tracked, it had many uses, and driving one around I kept wishing we'd had a few when we had been in France.

So I advanced from driving instructor and lecturer on motor vehicles to become the expert lecturing and explaining the mechanics and battle efficacy of the vehicle that was to become the workhorse of the war. Sometime later I was recommended for officer cadet training by Captain Beale, my superior officer. Despite his high opinion of me, I was found unsuitable, although I felt I performed reasonably well on the two-day testing that I had to attend. Neither Beale nor I were given any reason for the decision. However, because my political beliefs were well known and had been openly expressed throughout my service years, in conversations, discussions and debate, it was likely that this skewed the decision. My class background may have been also a factor in determining that I was not suitable officer material.

A large swathe of houses along the main promenade in Douglas had been commandeered as a detention camp for Italian nationals, most of whom had been living in Britain when war broke out and had been inadvertently caught up in the tragedy of war. Almost every morning I walked past the camp and received friendly greetings and more often than not, heard the familiar chords of an accordion being played, accompanied by the voice of one or more singers. The music was usually Italian, often choruses or arias from operas, about which I knew very little. It did, though, trigger in me a curiosity about all things Italian, something that played a significant role in my future life.

In my time on the Isle of Man I did have quite a lot of free time, and as there was no television in those days to distract me, I continued to read as much as possible. I was billeted in the house of a Mr. Dunbar, a butcher and local councillor, who was also chairman of the libraries committee. He never read any of the books that were regularly presented to him to decide on their suitability for inclusion in the public library. Once he had gathered that I enjoyed reading, he became a prolific source of new reading material for me. And, occasionally I was able to influence his choice of new books and it enabled me to infiltrate a few radical political volumes into the ultra-conservative Douglas library.

Lily was able to make infrequent visits and stayed one or two weeks. It was, though, an arduous and demanding journey for her. The seas were often rough for the ferry crossing and accommodation on board ship was minimal and the trains were little better. This was wartime and no emphasis was placed on comfort and luxury, at least not for the majority of us. However, once she arrived, the fact that we were able to be together even for such a short time was a great bonus. We had some great times cycling around the countryside on the island. For Lily this was also an opportunity to enjoy an abundance of food since the island had avoided the strict rationing imposed on the rest of the country, and was almost self-sufficient. Her special delicacy was toasted hard-boiled egg sandwiches.

On one occasion, while Lily was visiting, we became involved in a complex venture that I had dreamed up and then organised. It was towards the end of the war, at a period when I was concerned with soldiers' welfare — the provision of amenities and, in a small way, the protection of their rights.

In Douglas, the Villa Marina was renowned as the second largest ballroom in Europe. In its pre-war heyday, when many took their summer holidays on the island, it was crammed with couples, mostly from the north-western industrial centres, dancing their cares away to the music of leading big bands. Throughout the war it had been closed, so I approached the army authorities to see if we could open it up and hold a dance there. After protracted negotiations, and after providing numerous guarantees, the necessary approvals were given. We then negotiated with the ballroom management, booked the official band of the Royal Marines and a local big band to provide continuous music throughout the evening. We even reached agreement to open the seven bars and charged an entrance fee of a shilling and sixpence for servicemen, with a supplement of a further two shillings for civilians.

It was a tremendous success — the hall was packed to capacity. Lily and I spent all evening rushing from one entrance to the other, collecting entrance monies, checking turnstile numbers and then banking the money with the officer in charge. It was a great occasion and I received a tremendous accolade. We made more than sufficient profit to equip our own burgeoning band with a variety of instruments, and much more. That became my second organising venture.

Not long after that momentous event, another happened — Lily gave birth to our first child. Frances was born on May 13th, promisingly just one week after Armistice Day. I was in the woodwork shop when I was given the news. I was busy constructing a trolley, to carry coloured wooden blocks, and a wooden clothes horse. That was my limited contribution to the baby's birth and first few weeks of life, apart, of course, from my previous involvement in the conception.

CHAPTER ELEVEN
Back in Civvy Street and a Labour victory

VE Day was celebrated one week after Frances, my first child, a daughter, was born and it brought home to me, how much I wanted to return to civilian life again. Just before my demob, I was sent to Gloucester Barracks as a Sergeant Instructor. My duties there involved helping to set up a team of advisers and lecturers to help prepare soldiers for their demob. Among the earliest to be discharged would be the wounded and older men. However the barracks had been expanded to become a major holding base for many more troops awaiting demob. A programme had been developed as a form of induction to help soldiers, hardened and psychologically scarred by the war, adapt once again to 'civvy street', but it was yet to be put into full gear. At times it became difficult for us to cope with the sudden increase in numbers champing at the bit, waiting for their discharge.

Soon after my arrival, I made contact with a number of similarly minded, politically committed comrades. Once the election date — 5th July 1945 — had been declared, we took it upon ourselves to actively canvass for the election of a Labour government. A collective was formed from the among the various shades of the political left and centre-left, and communist party members were the most dedicated and determined among us. Our activities were, though, restricted by service regulations, but we nevertheless were able to distribute leaflets and raise the temperature of discussion in the barracks. We found fertile ground: some of the men had never been in full-time employment before they joined the army, and others had never belonged to a trades union. The majority was clearly determined that there should be no return to the old ways, and we were not afraid to give active encouragement to that view. No one doubted Churchill's wartime achievement and the leadership role he had played during the war, but the Tories would miscalculate if they thought his record would be enough to win them the peace. We were all proud of the contribution we were able to make to the resultant historic Labour victory. It was a time of renewed hope and personal aspiration – socialism was in the air.

Most of the courses offered as part of the induction process to smoothe the return to civilian life were vocational. Motor mechanics was one of the most popular courses, along with instruction in other manual trades, and these were my speciality. But I was also very much involved in teaching current affairs within the ABCA programme, and eventually I was authorised to open the debate on political subjects. Surprisingly, these lectures, debates and discussions were extremely popular and, although attendance was voluntary, good numbers came. The lecturers were drawn largely from the officer class, several of whom showed distinct liberal tendencies. I enjoyed this work since it gave me the opportunity of engaging in debate and argument at a higher level than I had been used to. At one particularly well attended, and heavy-going session we debated the government's decision to release Sir Oswald Mosley, the British fascist leader, from prison. The general and overwhelming consensus was opposed to his release. Had we all sacrificed some of the best years of our lives to defeat fascism only to see this Hitler-worshipper free to rebuild his fascist party again?

As March 1946 drew to a close, I was demobbed at last. But instead of returning home hale and hearty, I arrived on crutches! After managing to survive the whole war relatively unscathed, I fractured a leg playing football and, as a result of a faulty diagnosis, it was not recognised until only a few days before my demobilisation date. I was given the option of deferring my release or going home in plaster. I had no hesitation in choosing the latter and returned as an 'injured soldier'. I wallowed in the sympathy I received, but not without feeling a smidgin of guilt.

Now that I was home, there was the responsibility of fatherhood and, of course, marriage, both requiring considerable adjustments to my way of life and behaviour. It was not easy, and I'm sure other demobbed soldiers found the same. Lily and I had not spent more than two continuous weeks together throughout the whole war period and under completely different circumstances. Lily's mother had died the year previously, as much from exhaustion caused by the rigours of surviving the hardships of war, after having already suffered the trauma of emigration from Romania at a young age, as well as an early marriage, producing seven children, and then widowed when still young.

Over our years together, Lily has been a considerable influence and support. She and the children often helped me in my political activities and business work, doing the usual folding and disribution of leaflets. She rarely opposed what I intended to do, despite being pressurised by outside influences. We discussed my decisions into the early hours, but there was only one time that she made a negative comment and that was when I signed my first holiday charter. Lying in bed, she said: 'for the first time in our lives you're working (as a cabbie) and earning a good living why do you want to do this?' I told her it was what I felt I had to do, and she replied: 'fine let's do it then'. Lily was adaptable, surprisingly so, and was never duanted by titled or powerful individulals. She mixed with all sorts, but always made it very clear to them that she supported my views, including my socialist beliefs, which were never hidden.

With the birth of our baby, Lily had left work to devote herself full-time to motherhood and managing the home. Two of her brothers also returned to the family home and expected her to replace the mother who for years had served them hand and foot, then there was me to look after. For weeks I found it very difficult to adjust to this new life.

My father, whose business had prospered during the war, and with the opportunities to gamble temporarily restricted, had become quite affluent. Taking full advantage of the upturn in business due to the general food shortages, had also given him the opportunity to consolidate his new-found wealth. But, although, I couldn't work in the first few months, as a consequence of my broken leg, he had no intention of re-employing me as the law dictated he should. He objected to the principles he assumed I still held – and he was right about that – he was of the view that I might object to participating in his illegal activities. My parents continued, as they had throughout the war, refusing us any support whatsoever during this difficult period and despite my daughter being their only grandchild.

When my leg came out of plaster, I was offered a job as a long-distance lorry driver, which I did for two years. I delivered furniture and carpets to northern towns like Halifax, Wakefield and Liverpool. This required night driving and days away from home. After our long period of separation, neither Lily nor I were happy about this. Nevertheless, when I learned that my father was terminally ill I gave in to pressure from my mother and returned to run the business. I did so with very mixed feelings. I wasn't exactly enamoured with the long hours and time away from home that driving entailed, so was not too reluctant to give it up. I also hoped that the change in my father's health would perhaps alter his demeanour and soften his animosity towards me. After much consideration, and with the need to do something different as soon as possible, I accepted. Despite everything, the ties of blood and a feeling of family loyalty held sway. But even these were eventually eroded by the gambling curse that still blighted his life.

My parents, Dora and Ike, in the late thirties.

My mother was, at this time, an ailing woman herself and had been so for some years. She suffered from kidney stones, and in those days the only cure was to operate. These she had to undergo on several occasions and each time her pain was more excruciating. My father was diagnosed with advanced cancer just before my mother herself died. The medical profession eventually found the cause of her problem, it was actually in the thyroid. The doctors decided to operate on the gland which was causing calcium to be removed from her bones and then passed through the kidneys.

The operation was successful except that her body was incapable of making the sudden and necessary adjustment. She continued to suffer the most excruciating pain. My father, far advanced in his illness, nevertheless continued his normal routine, taking cash from the till and ignoring the mounting pile of bills. Even in his dire physical state, drugged-up to his eyeballs, he was still unable to resist a visit to the gambling joints, particularly the Little Somerset Club in Aldgate, where the vultures awaited this easy meat, clearing him out of whatever monies he had. He had no compunction about calling me in the small hours of the morning to collect him and drive him home. Sometimes to his house in Finchley, but just as often to our home where Lily looked after him. Eventually, in 1950, he too died, a painful death.

CHAPTER TWELVE
Becoming a Cabby

M y father made a will, an unusual thing in those days for a man of his generation to do. The business was to be divided equally between the eldest of my sisters and me. Her husband suggested that I buy her out and pay £4,000 for her share. My reply was a tirade of expletives. I decided it was time I moved on, and I just walked away from the business. That was in the latter part of 1950.

All that we inherited was a small sum of money that had come to me from the sale of my parents' house, which had been owned by my mother and because probate had not been cleared, it had not passed into my father's hands. The grand sum was £417 and 10 shillings, hardly a fortune, but welcome nevertheless. Since the birth of our son, we now had two children, and I had no desire either to stay in baking or to return to long distance lorry driving. In the end, after some deliberation, I chose to follow my brother-in-law, Sam, and become a London black cab driver, as a number of my contemporaries had done.

But before I was allowed to join the select few, I had to 'do the knowledge', a task that then required at least a year of full-time daily grind on a pushbike around the streets of the city and then, in the evening, 'cottoning up' the next day's journeys so that they were integrated and no unnecessary time was lost. Then, on top of this, were the monthly visits to the offices of the relevant Metropolitan Police station, in my case the one in Lambeth Road, to have my progress monitored. The whole procedure was an awesome task, particularly in my precarious financial circumstances. Nevertheless Lily agreed that I should do it and I set myself a target of nine months before I would be on the road.

The Met provided me with the ominous Blue Book containing hundreds of journeys criss-crossing London and with prominent departure and arrival points. I had my first appointment with the police four weeks after registering. These would start early in the morning and finish at midday. They consisted of driving with a police inspector in the back. The officer conducting my inquisition was the forbidding Inspector McKie, and I had to answer all his questions. In the beginning the questions were strictly according to the runs as described in the Blue Book, but as you improved, other points surrounding the originals would be used and the time between appointments reduced. I was required to explain exactly how I would get from one point to the other, naming every street and where to turn left or right.

I had to buy a second-hand pushbike in order to practise the routes. Once I'd finished, I sold it to the playwright, Arnold Wesker's mother for five shillings. It enabled him to get to his work in a kitchen, a place that provided him with the raw material for his renowned play of the same name.

A few days after I'd started my course, I met a young man, Alf Coleman, who was also 'doing the knowledge' and lived on the same estate as us, so we joined forces. We worked extremely hard; we were out on our push bikes early in the morning, in every sort of weather and then 'cottoning up' in the evenings and late into the night, in preparation for the next day's runs. 'Cottoning up' involved laying a large map on the table or floor and placing one end of a length of cotton thread on the departure point and the other on the destination. All traversable roads along that line determined the route to be taken. The next day we would make the journey noting the one-ways, which were far fewer then at present, but equally important, and noting any outstanding or important buildings.

Once you had established, both in your own mind and that of the inspector's, that you had a comprehensive knowledge of the basic runs, it was important to memorise prominent places around each Blue Book point and several that were on the way. I began to spend mornings in the nearby café, Marcantonios, where we trainees would gather to exchange points and grill those who had just come out of the tests. I worked diligently and successfully, passing out in just six months, two weeks and one day, well within the target period I had set myself. I received my bill and the badge number 2176. I was very proud of my achievement, for in that era a full-timer couldn't normally expect to do the course in less than a year, at the very least.

On my first day as a 'cabby', I took the bus at five in the morning from Stamford Hill to 'Lord' Johnny Nelson's garage in Richmond Road, adjacent to Mare Street in Hackney. I picked up my cab and then drove in a long line of like-minded cabbies down Pentonville Road to King's Cross where I spent over an hour waiting for the 'Irish' train to come in. My first fare was a matronly lady of obvious wealth, her clothing adorned with fur trimmings, and, as if to prove her affluence, asked to be taken to 36 Grosvenor Street in Mayfair. The fare was one shilling and sixpence and I received a threepenny tip. Still I was back working.

If for some reason I was late starting work, I would invariably put on the cab rank at Ashwin Street, opposite Dalston Junction railway station. There was a café on the corner and I, along with other cabbies, would go in for tea or coffee or just to shelter from the cold. It was in this café that I renewed my acquaintance with Lionel Begleiter who was a member of my party branch. Lionel had spent considerable time with the left-wing Unity Theatre in the years before the war, and was now involved with Joan Littlewood's famous Theatre Workshop in Stratford East. Later, as Lionel Bart, he was to write successful and well-loved musicals including *Fings Ain't Wot They Used To Be, Lock Up Your Daughters* and, the best of all, the music and lyrics to *Oliver*. Lionel introduced me to a red-haired, bearded chap called John Gorman. They were partners running a silk screen-printing business with premises in Rokesby Street. John and I later became the greatest of friends.

CHAPTER THIRTEEN
I stand as a communist candidate

Although I had retained my belief in socialism since the war, and over the years had been close to a number of communists particularly at Gloucester Barracks, I never joined the party. Like so many like-minded friends of mine, I was exhilarated by, and welcomed the Labour victory of 1945, for which I'd worked incessantly. But I still recall my anguish and disappointment at the reasons and the manner of my having to leave the Labour Party.

After my demob I immediately became involved in the formation of a tenants' association on the Stamford Hill Estate, whose landlord was the London County Council. Because of my irregular and unsocial hours as a lorry driver, I was somewhat limited in terms of the work I could devote to the association, but that didn't stop them making me secretary. I was, of course, 'elected' in the usual fashion, being the only willing fool to allow my nomination to go forward! Once my hours became more regular, though, I became more deeply involved and was instrumental in the setting up of a youth club and a ladies' keep-fit class, but most of the work involved dealing with the numerous problems that arose daily on an estate of that size.

Tenants' associations were formed on many estates after the war and were instrumental in making sure vital repair and renovation work was done, that landlords were held accountable, as well as dealing with the myriad minor disputes or problems that arose. Really, they were often doing the job that should have been done by the landlords. Sadly, many Labour councils, instead of welcoming the work these truly grassroots organisations did and working in partnership with them, invariably saw them as a thorn in their side and deliberately circumvented or ignored them.

As secretary of our association, I experienced first hand the party political machinations and the difficulties and frustrations this caused us. There were a large number of active Labour Party members living on the estate, and one Hackney Labour councillor in particular, but all shunned the association. It appeared that a directive from above had warned them not to have anything to do with us, that we were politically 'suspect'. Looking after the well-being of its members, the coming together of tenants, particularly in London, was seen to be creating problems for the London County Council, which was then controlled by Labour. In particular the aggressive Mrs. Dennington who, as Director of Housing in the administration, was very much the archetypal battle axe and very unhelpful towards us.

The usual tenant problems were repairs, decorating, caretaking and cleaning, and we were continually badgering the council on these, insisting on the work being done and promptly. The retention of the underground shelters was also an ongoing and contentious issue. Children, including my own son, used to play and climb in them, often falling and injuring themselves. The number of protest letters to the council mounted, but little was done in response.

The frustration at such lack of response and the often supercilious attitude our Labour representatives took, pushed me toward the local Communist Party branch whose members were active in raising and pursuing these issues and were always ready to help. Among them was Mrs. 'Bron', whose son became the noted scientist and television personality, Jacob Bronowski, and Alec Franks, a jovial academically-minded dry cleaner with whom I found myself working ever more closely. Eventually, following the sudden death of Alec and the cancellation at 24 hours notice of an election in which he was standing, I decided to join the communists.

Soon I was deeply involved in local party activity and eventually stood as a candidate in several election battles, both for the local council and for the LCC. On three occasions I was partnered by Frank Chapple, a not very active communist, but because of his party membership, he hmanaged to get elected as an official in the then largely communist-dominated Electrical Trades Union. After being instrumental in helping to topple the communist leadership after a vote-rigging scandal and a vicious media campaign to smash communist domination of this key union, Chapple was later rewarded with a lordship.

Although nominally a member of the House of Lords, he receded from public view and was politically inactive until he died in 2004. On one occasion an electoral opponent of mine was Neville Sandleson, a wealthy lawyer standing for

Labour who, although virtually unknown locally won the council election easily and then proceeded to make 21 attempts to be adopted as a prospective MP. He was eventually successful in Hayes and Harlington, but left Labour to join the breakaway SDLP and eventually the Conservatives, before disappearing into oblivion.

I became the Communist Party candidate for the parliamentary constituency of Stoke Newington and Hackney North in the 1955 election. David Weitzman was the incumbent Labour MP. He was a man who liked a quiet life. A Barrister, he was chosen at a time when the constituency was changing with an influx into the area of working class people, and a growing proportion of East London Jews. It was the end of the long-standing Conservative hierarchy of Colonel Loweth, a local building magnate, and his cronies.

Of course I was defeated just as I had been in earlier local elections. But the campaign was exhilarating. i would speak at large gatherings, like the one with Harry Pollitt (then General Secretary of the CPGB) at Skinners School to 1,000 people and with Willy Gallagher, the first elected Communist MP in Britain, at Tyssen School. Willy, by then no longer in parliament, and because of his age, somewhat handicapped physically, stayed with us in our flat overnight. He had a fund of stories with which he regaled us, laced with his wonderfully dry, Scottish humour. Despite his heavy Scots accent, which made him difficult to understand, our children, Frances and Michael, found him a fascinating character.

Around this time, I first met Solly Kaye and his wife Margaret. Solly was then a full time worker for the Communist Party and had also stood in local elections on several occasions. He was eventually elected and became the leader of the Communist group of four councillors on Stepney council. He was a tireless activist as well as an eloquent and inspiring public speaker. He epitomised the hero of Roger McGough's poem *Blessed are the Agitators*. Margaret, his wife, was from Bishop Auckland and from a staunch communist family. Our friendship endured the many disagreements and changes in political lines and allegiances that came about over the succeeding years.

My electoral agent was Jack Sutherland, a Scot from Aberdeen. He was an experienced politician but much more importantly, he was an honest one. University educated, he helped me understand clearly the way politics worked, and most particularly, how to distinguish between the relevant and the irrelevant or unimportant, and this served me well in later life. We became good friends and had many things in common: a love of jazz was one, and a certain cynicism towards the London leadership of the party was another. He gave me pointers as to what was worth reading, introducing me to a wider field of literature, drama and the theatre, for which I am still grateful. It was during that election campaign

Local bazaar to raise money for the *Daily Worker*, circa 1950.

that he met and courted Doreen Hoyland (formerly Williams), who had been a leading member of the Labour Party League of Youth and *Advance*.

Our failure to move sufficient numbers of people to vote for the Communist Party, put in the general context of national and international events, could be understood. It was, though, galling to learn that at grassroots level, no matter how hard I worked organising in the local community, representing constituents and dealing with their problems — and however distant and uninterested the Labour Party was in dealing with these same problems — old and established loyalties remained unshakeable.

Once our daughter, Frances, reached eleven, she had to take the 11-plus selective exam, as did all other children on the estate. This exam, based on spurious measures of 'intelligence', was clearly biased in favour of middle class children and was, years later, revealed as seriously flawed. But for generations of children who grew up during that period it wreaked enormous damage, condemning the majority to a second-rate secondary education, while propelling a small elite into grammar schools and a better start in later life.

Throughout the electoral campaigns at all levels, I argued the case for comprehensive schools, to give every child a chance and overcome the unfairness of the selective system. A major plank in our campaign had been the need to extend this new concept, and nearby we had the second of such purpose built comprehensive schools at Woodberry Down — a fine example for all to see, but there was little interest. A Grammar School place remained the objective for those looking for upward mobility. It was ironic, that although there was little interest in my campaign, the morning after the II-plus results were announced, a queue built up outside our top floor flat of people asking me how they could get their failed children into Woodberry Down! Frances was one of the few children on our estate who passed the II-plus, and was the only one to attend Woodberry from where she went on to university, as did our son, Michael, some four years later. Despite these policy setbacks I continued to give time to the Party but eased up in my work for the Residents' Association.

CHAPTER FOURTEEN
I buy my own cab

In 1953 I was in the enviable position to borrow the necessary £200 deposit on one of the first diesel taxicabs, and joined the privileged, as a 'mush'- an owner. The remaining sum, a formidable amount, was to be paid back over three years.

The life of a self-employed cabbie has one very determining aspect: if you don't work, you don't eat; it's as simple as that! However, an advantage is that you can arrange your work to fit in with your own personal life and the energies you have. I worked alongside a group of young drivers, all unmarried, who worked long night hours throughout the summer and then spent the whole winter in Las Palmas, in the Canaries, recuperating and relaxing in style. Renting a room for ten shillings a week, they lived in the sun for almost six months of the year, while others with families, mortgages and children, who worked just as hard, barely scraped through. There were also those who worked merely their regular hours and others who simply did the minimum, whenever it was convenient. I worked regular hours, and while I did not enjoy the work, I respected the certain freedom the job gave me. We had a choice of working night or day, the area in which we wished to work, the hours we wanted to put in and when and where we had lunch.

There was a great camaraderie and banter among most of the drivers. We were a tightly knit community, often from similar backgrounds, many of us Jewish East-Enders, and we felt a strong affinity with each other. 'New on the rank?' someone would ask, and immediately begin chatting.

If you were quick off the mark, there were also unlikely opportunities to seize upon. I recall with some satisfaction, in October 1958, reading an article in the

Daily Express by that doyen of sports writers, Desmond Hackett, telling readers that it was impossible to get near the first Soviet Union soccer team to visit England. They had arrived to play a friendly at Wembley. A short time later, I found myself on the rank at the Athenaeum Hotel in Piccadilly and saw a group of men leaving the hotel who looked to me like Russians as well as soccer players. I found a scrap of paper in the car and approached one for his autograph, to which he not only agreed but also took me in to see the team coach, where I obtained autographs of the entire group. I came off the rank and drove to Fleet Street, and asked to see Hackett and, rather belligerently as I recall, thrust the paper under his nose. He read it, said thank you most politely, but nothing more. However, the very next day the story was on the front page!

It's a cliché, but holds some truth, that most cabbies have failed in other jobs — in academia, on the stage or have been generally frustrated in their previous employment — and this certainly applied to me. Driving a cab was a last resort, but also the first opportunity to be commercially successful. It also gave, those that wanted it, the flexible hours and freedom to undertake other interests or careers. Charley Poulson was an erudite working class lad, who wrote historical novels and incisive political papers while employed as a cabbie. The work gave him the freedom and opportunity he needed to write and to think, while at the same time providing the necessary income. Graham Benjamin, apart from the time he devoted to running laps around Paddington recreation ground, studied for and obtained a law degree while still working as a cabbie. This was a favoured option. There were also professional gamblers and part time bookies on the rank. Ron Philips introduced the concept of London walking holidays from Aldgate Station. Others supplemented their income as part-time street traders or in other professions. A number also became local councillors and one, Lou Sherman, was eventually knighted by a Labour government for his political work.

Whenever possible I would have my light lunch at Angelo's in Panton Street, off Leicester Square, in a small, narrow shop close to the Comedy Theatre. There was no seating, just a narrow ledge that ran the length of one wall, on which to rest tea cups and elbows while standing. It was one of many similar watering holes used by the cabbies. There were always regulars there and it would be a special day if the conversation meandered far from moans about traffic congestion, miserly tippers, football and crusty passengers. On occasions, though, we did discuss more worldly issues and had arguments, usually about politics or sport, which would sometimes become quite heated. We had one elderly and horny driver who regaled us with his fantasies about the women he carried in his cab. His perceptive powers describing their physical attributes and sexual abilities were outdone only by his crude, pornographic descriptions of his own

PUV 172, my first black cab and affectionately called 'my droshky', 1954.

prowess and amorous conquests. He, predictably, was given the sobriquet 'Casanova'. Others had their nick-names too: 'Ananias' the congenital liar, and 'Nuts and Bolts' who could always provide the necessary technical assistance needed in an emergency. We often didn't know their real names. The major reference point would be to a particular quirk or, more usually, their cab number. Me, I was known as 'Red' and that didn't refer to the colour of my hair!

Over the years, the old cab shelters disappeared one after the other, but they were still used by the heavy eaters with time to spare. Full breakfast, lunch or dinner, good food served in the atmosphere of an old fashioned working men's café. Here the conversation would often be more personal and often jovial.

The advantage being a cab driver was that through conversations with your fares you picked up a lot of information, trivial, useless and interesting. During my working hours I learned a lot about the better restaurants, good theatres and which films to see. It was through my fares, for instance, that I learned about the wonderful Italian neo-realist films that were showing in town.

In the last months of the war Lily, who had always been a keen filmgoer, went to the cinema once every week. This she continued to do even after I came back home; we had few opportunities to go together while the children were young, so one of us had to stay behind and baby-sit. With the election campaign over and my involvement in the tenants' association now a looser one, Lily and I ventured outside our own patch, and were captivated by such films as Rosselini's *Rome Open City* and de Sica's *Bicycle Thieves,* De Santi's *Bitter Harvest* and Fellini's

La Strada. These were films that introduced a new and vibrant sense of real life into what was largely tinselly Hollywood or Ealing escapism. They showed the harsh lives of working people, told moving and dramatic stories and got under your skin.

These films also encouraged us to visit some of the new Italian restaurants that popped up as from nowhere. Our particular favourite was the popular Spaghetti House in Goodge Street. Italian songs, like *Volare*, also became popular on the radio. All of this must have influenced me to start learning Italian. From then on, much of my waiting time on the ranks was spent studying Italian grammars and conversation manuals. Holborn library also had a large collection of Italian literature, and I was soon trying to read books in Italian with the help of a dictionary. I practised my newfound skills on Angelo and his wife Wanda, at the café. They were always happy to exchange niceties with me and I soon managed to acquire a reasonable vocabulary.

Italian food, clothes and films soon became all the rage, certainly in London and the south. Cappuccinos replaced that milky washing up water that so often in Britain posed as coffee, and hot chocolate. Lily and I, with the children too, became very partial to all things Italian.

CHAPTER FIFTEEN
By London cab to the continent

In the fifties, few working class people travelled abroad. Most hadn't travelled far beyond where they lived, apart from, perhaps, the odd few days in one of the better known holiday resorts: Clacton, Skegness or Blackpool. The idea of package holidays and cheap travel were not even on the horizon.

The year of the general election in 1955, my friend Joe Morrison, by now established as a certified accountant, decided to take his family abroad on a motoring holiday and discussed it with us at great length. I was intrigued by the idea and after days of family debate I decided that this was what I would also like to do. The question was how − we had no car and really had no surplus money. But then I realised that there was, of course, the cab, and I could put in a few extra hours to increase our income. We should be able to manage, providing we kept the cost of hotels to a minimum.

I checked with the Carriage Office (the licensing authority) whether it could be done, and whether anyone had done it before and if so who? (I felt a little advice would be invaluable). I was told it had never been done before, but yes, I could do it, provided I handed in my registration plate − the white square plate on the rear of the cab, and my meter, before departure. I would also have to be prepared to undergo a repeat of the compulsory rigorous test normally required of a new cab and the annual overhaul all cabs undergo, before I could again ply for hire on my return. This was an enormous disincentive and meant a lot of heart searching. At this time, I was earning a living, but no more, and I was reluctant to jeopardise my livelihood for an adventure into the unknown. Should the vehicle need major, or even minor repairs sufficient to keep me off the road for any length of time, I would be unable to earn any money and the result would be disastrous.

My mates viewed my planned undertaking with genuine disbelief; certainly misgivings, though some of them, probably with envy. They lost no time warning me of the possible consequences to my living if things went pear-shaped. Nevertheless they gave me lots of help, lending me a tent and other small, but vital items of equipment. There were those, of course, who thought I was plain bonkers and didn't mince their words in telling me so. Lily agreed to accompany me, but also with considerable apprehension; the children, understandably, saw it as a fantastic adventure – I think?!

Lily, the children and I, were soon totally gripped by this big idea of a foreign trip and we spent several evenings avidly debating the pros and cons of the undertaking. We were entering uncharted territory! In the end, Lily and I, with rising excitement, decided that since we both worked hard and really wanted to go, we'd go for it and take any consequences on the nose. We felt we were entitled to a holiday like this, and such opportunities should be grabbed when they arise.

£100 maximum outgoings were my target, so taking camping gear would be a vital necessity. Neither of us had ever gone camping for leisure; my only experience was sleeping in an army tent at Bulford Camp, but I'd never had to put one up. We certainly couldn't afford to buy a tent and we knew no one from whom we could borrow. So I let it be known on the cab ranks what we intended to do, and soon afterwards the offers came in, one of which we accepted. The tent we were loaned was a little woebegone, white and flimsy contraption that had obviously seen better days, but the main criterion was that it would sleep us all. Our other items of luggage, cooking utensils and heating equipment would go on the roof-rack. We had no idea what items were essential for such a journey, as we were complete novices. There were also very few people, in those days, to whom we could go for advice.

Up until this madcap adventure, we had had few opportunities for holidays, apart from a single week each year. Once I became established in the cab trade, we saved for our annual week's holiday at Westbrook, a tiny resort adjacent to Margate, with a wide, sandy beach nearby. We would travel by coach from George Ewer's garage opposite the flats and head for Mrs. Feldman's guest house where we occupied a large room at the top of the house. We went full-board, which included a good English breakfast, a three course lunch and high tea, of either beans or eggs on toast with chunks of bread, taken at 6pm. Before bed-time there would be hot cocoa. Minnie Feldman was an industrious, shrewd, but likeable lady. At first there were just ourselves and our friends, the Lewis's, who'd been recommended to stay there, but soon relatives and friends took over the whole house on that particular week each year.

Westbrook was an ideal resort, with huts directly on the beach. These weren't easy to rent, but were an obvious asset on Britain's often cold and wind-swept coasts. To rent one, you had to apply at least one year in advance, and we always reserved our week at Minnie's for the following year on our day of departure.

The resort boasted ice cream stands all over the place and donkey rides, if the weather was good, but more often than not it wasn't! From the window of our one large room containing the three beds, each morning, the first thing we did was to look out to see if we could see the fort further down the coast. If we could, then the day would invariably be great, otherwise it would be pretty grim. The holiday we now planned was a whole different ball game and, understandably, we were not a little scared.

The following weeks we spent poring over guide books and maps loaned from the public library. The gathering excitement of the adventure overcame our fears and trepidation and having decided where we intended to head for, the routes and names of places soon became as familiar as those in the cabbies' Blue Book.

Our close friends, the Morrisons, who would join us in Italy, decided to travel to the South of France directly and then on to the Italian Riviera. For us it had to be the quickest route into Italy. We would head for Milan and then on to Genoa, where we had agreed with them that whichever family arrived first would leave a message at the main post office, so that we could meet up.

Our route would take us through Northern France into Switzerland and over the St. Gothard Pass, into Milan, where, by chance, I had a contact: a young Italian who with his wife had lived nearby in Stamford Hill and had been a constant visitor to our flat. When they returned home to live in Milan they left their address and telephone number with the usual 'come and visit us whenever you are down our way'. Of course neither they nor we envisaged at the time that it would ever happen, but two years' later we intended to take up the invitation. We had no intention of staying with them, but hoped to obtain guidance from a 'local' regarding the best beach resorts where we could camp.

There were looks of complete disbelief from both passengers and crew as our London black cab was driven across the lowered stern of the Lord Vernon ferry at Dover. They must have thought some very rich patron was taking a cab to the Continent or, perhaps, that it had been stolen!

It entered the noisy, smelly belly of the ship and joined the motley collection of cars and trucks with their passengers and cargo on the sea voyage across the Channel to Boulogne. My taxi, even without the clock and plate, and despite the large and cumbersome roof rack, still looked elegant, spotless and unmistakeable. It certainly fuelled the gossip on board and our children were endlessly quizzed by the curious, but they revelled in the attention.

We felt we were real pioneers and, with the first modest stage of our journey under way, we began to relax and enjoy the crossing. Frances aged ten and Michael six, soon adapted to the adventure, quickly finding and reporting on all the various facilities and the people on board. For Lily and me it was an opportunity to reflect and realise that after all the months of hard work, anxiety and trepidation we were finally on our way. We didn't give much thought to what lay ahead, the main thing was, we were doing it.

Our objective was to reach Italy as soon as we could. We planned our return journey along the Italian and French Rivieras at a much more leisurely pace, when we would know how much time and money, if any, we had left. The whole trip was to take approximately three weeks and to cost no more than just £100.

Strangely I was not bothered about language problems. I had accumulated an Italian vocabulary of sorts, enough, I thought, to get by. I had also done two years of elementary French at school. It had already been of some, if limited, use during the Dunkirk campaign. It was, though, somewhat unfortunate that my French teacher had been born and spent most of her life in County Cork, in Ireland and her strong Irish accent had been adopted by me when speaking French. Most of the French people with whom I tried to communicate appeared not to understand me at all, and this sapped any confidence I had, but it did get better over the days.

Our first stop was in the town of Arras. During my brief sojourn in France with the British Expeditionary Force, as it was so grandly named, I had made several visits to the city on evening nights out. As I was responsible for the vehicles, I had had little opportunity of acquainting myself with the general layout except of the square close to the town hall where the vehicles were parked. Anyway, it was obvious that in the few years that had passed, reconstruction works had made it unrecognisable. Resolutely, we followed the road signs directing us to the campsite which was on an island. This had obviously been a bombsite, of which there were still very many, and had been cleaned up and equipped with the bare necessities. It was free, however, and that was encouraging. The thought of camping was a constant cloud over my head and we soon learned how difficult it could be.

As we entered, we were stunned by the array of colourful tents laid out in neat, serried ranks, mostly orange in colour, spacious and lavishly equipped with separate bedrooms and lounges. We were suddenly made ashamed of the lily-white, ghostly apparition that was ours, and debated whether we should leave and put it up out of sight. We decided that it would be little different wherever we went, and eventually overcame our embarrassment. After a few mishaps, we managed to erect our ramshackle bivouac. It had looked so wonderful when we had tried it out in my sister's back garden, but here it was something of an eyesore. The ground was rock hard and it took some hard work to drive in the pegs. Once it was up, though, we managed to prepare a meal, then went to bed tucked up in our borrowed sleeping bags. Thoroughly exhausted, we slept the sleep of the just.

Contrary to what we had been led to believe, the ablution and toilet facilities were more than sufficient, although the tepid showers were not what we would have chosen for an early morning start. We had breakfast with fresh, crispy bread from a nearby bakery, then, with lots of directions and advice from our fellow campers, we continued our trek. As we progressed across France, the country-side became increasingly attractive. The children had plenty of space in the cab, but Lily spent most of the time seated on the pull-down bucket seat behind me while I was driving. I had opened the partition window-wide and, in this way, we could converse.

Our next overnight stop was on the outskirts of Belfort where, having purchased an abundant supply of baguettes, cheeses and wine to go with the vorsht (Jewish salami), we had a splendid evening meal. The weather was now warm and pleasant and, later, huddled together we spent a comfortable night.

Arriving at Aosta in the foothills of the Alps, we had two alternatives routes: we could join a long queue to go through the toll tunnel or drive over the pass. The former would use up some of our very limited cash and it would also mean we would miss traversing our first real mountain range, so in our naivety we chose the latter route.

Initially the climb was steady, the road undulating and without problematic bends. The weather was all we had hoped for and our means of transport was behaving well. The air was invigorating, we were relaxed and there was not very much traffic; and what there was diminished as the road became steeper. We noticed that there was a lot of repair work being carried out on the road but this did not worry us unduly. We were more fascinated by the numerous pastel-brown cows with their big brass bells tinkling pleasingly in the stillness.

The climb soon became more and more difficult and our pace progressively slower and, as the hours passed, we began to worry whether we would find some-where to pitch our tent for the night. Eventually we did reach the top, and encountered a dramatic change from the comparatively easy miles that we'd traversed. We entered what seemed like an enormous construction site, with trucks and excavating machines. Men were suspended from cables on the mountain, and the road was largely covered with wooden slats and piles of gravel. We tagged on to a line of traffic waiting to cross a bridge, and watched as a stream of cars came from the other side.

After some time, and it was by now becoming quite dark and cold, we were allowed to move forward only to find that the actual bridge consisted of loosely placed wooden slats, beneath which the deep void gaped menacingly below us. We had to drive extremely slowly and were more than gratified once we reached firm land again, leaving the makeshift bridge behind us. However, by this time it was now pitch black, and we were exhausted and burnt out. It was certainly time to settle down for the night, but where? We came across an open space by the roadside, and prepared to put up the tent. It was then that my total inadequacy in camping matters was fully exposed.

We could see very little in the intense blackness, so put on the taxi's headlights. These, of course, attracted whole swarms and every variety of insect imaginable. Putting up the tent in the stiff wind, which tore at its fabric, while swotting the unwelcome beasts, was beyond me − we despaired. Defeated, we all bundled back into the cab and, using every possible cover, settled down till the early light woke us.

What I had thought in the dark was a large open space to camp, in the daylight turned out to be something very different. If we'd driven only a few yards further it would have been disastrous, as we had parked virtually on the edge of a precipice. We departed with little ado to seek a safer spot to have our breakfast. We both marvelled that we'd managed the journey this far, but bemoaned our lack of sleep and hunger. We discarded any ideas we might have entertained of returning home this way.

On the outskirts of Milan we stopped to examine our map of the city, trying to pinpoint my friend, Franco's apartment. This was extremely difficult, but with a little patience, lots of questioning and an amazing amount of luck, we found him. Franco and his wife were really taken aback when they opened the door. It was easy to appreciate that their offer of hospitality had been made in the belief that it would never be taken up. We soon dispelled their fears, that we had perhaps come to stay, and enjoyed fresh coffee, pannetoni, while they gave us suggestions as to the places we should visit and what would best suit my preconceived ides of real Italian resorts.

'Go to Marina da Massa', said Franco 'That's the ideal place for you', and he pointed to a tiny spot on the coast, south of Genoa close to the better known Viarregio. We had agreed with our friends the Morrisons that Genoa would be our contact point. Genoa was not an easy place for strangers, even more difficult than Milan, but after some minor problems we got there and found that we were ahead of them, so left a note containing onward directions, as we understood them.

We continued our journey along the Mediterranean coast. The road was hazardous, but the beauty around us was overwhelming and there was, thankfully, very little traffic. It was only later that we learned that we now had 'Ferragusta' behind us – the last two weeks of July and first two in August – when all Italians take their holidays. We drove gently through St. Margherita and, overwhelmed by the ambience, decided to look for a hotel for the night and take in the beauty of the area in relaxed style.

Rapallo seemed an ideal place to camp, but my limited Italian frustrated my attempt to understand the answer to what I believed was a question in impeccable Italian. So we drove on to Chiavari, where we found a camp site on the beach. The next morning, awakened by the sound of the incoming tide lapping around us, we jumped out of our sacks and fled to dry ground. Just another example of our lack of camping experience! We went for a long walk around the town, to give our equipment time to dry out, and were fascinated by all that we saw.

At last, we were savouring the real Italy that up to now had only been a fantasy in our heads. On the cool piazza, lined with shops and shaded by cloistered archways, the memories of the long drive along the endless ribbon of road shimmering in the midday heat were banished from our thoughts, and our first restaurant meal, we felt, was a foretaste of pleasures to come.

Reluctantly leaving Chiavari, we headed for Massa. Then, approaching Sarzana we saw banners stretched across the road with the words 'Festa de L'Unita' (a festival of *l'Unita*, the communist party daily) emblazoned across them. Lily and I were thrilled – this we had to experience. We hadn't travelled all this way to miss an opportunity like this of contacting politically like-minded people. We could already hear the music in the distance, so we parked the cab and joined the crowd, trying to locate someone who spoke English. Meanwhile we enjoyed the food on offer, particularly the crispy pescalini, my first taste of whitebait. As soon as they were caught, they were tossed into the hot oil and served in small white paper bags.

Eventually we found a local teacher of English, and through him we were able to converse with fellow socialists and communists. We were regaled with stories of the resistance movement in the area and of the vital battle in the nearby Bracco Pass, when a large contingent of Nazi troops were beaten by a much smaller force of resistance guerrillas We were given the name of Allessandro, who had been one of those resistance leaders, and who lived in Carrara. 'How do we find him?', I asked. 'Just mention his name, everyone will know', they replied.

Reluctantly, we left the festivities and drove on until we reached Massa where the only hotel we could see was the commercial Albergo Centrico where we were provided with a large room containing a 'letto matrimoniale' (matrimonial bed) which could easily have held all four of us, plus several more. There were also two other beds in the room, and a bathroom nearby with a proper toilet. Our long day was finished off with a substantial and tasty meal, after which we had our first night in a proper bed after days of makeshift.

Probably the most inconvenient and uncomfortable aspect so far had been the malodorous, 'crouch' toilets, which were the only ones available during the whole of our journey. One excellent thing that the later tourist expansion did was to rid the country of these unpleasant 'conveniences'.

The next morning, after a modest continental breakfast, we headed for the beach and miles of glorious golden sand. With the help of my treasured diction-ary we gathered that to use the beach we had to purchase space and the facili-ties of deckchairs, umbrellas and use of showers from one of the many 'bagni-nos'. We chose a spot with a frontal and prominent parking space for our cab (essential if the Morrisons were ever to find us!).

The person in charge of the 'bagno' was a charming young woman with a babe in arms who looked after us very well and was helpful in every way. The beaches were of fine sand and the sea was amazingly warm. There were just a few Italian families around with whose children Frances and Michael soon found common interests. We swam, played and relaxed.

One evening, on returning to the hotel, Lily noticed that her wrist-watch was gone. We concluded that it had been lost on the beach. I dashed back hoping to find it, but to no avail. The Signora, with various gestures, told me to wait till the morning. Sure enough, it had been found by the man who swept the beach each morning, and handed in. Honesty among ordinary people was still very much a tradition in those pre-acquisitive days. We were overjoyed to have it back.

The Morrisons arrived two days later, spotted the cab in front of the hotel and joined us. We went on to spend eleven glorious days together. Evenings were usu-ally spent strolling around the streets of Massa. In the town square we joined small crowds sharing the joys and sorrows of a La Scala performance of *La Bohème* on one of the few tiny televisions then available, while sipping our coffees in one of the many open air cafes. A trip into Viareggio in my cab aroused local curiosity, and I was asked if I knew various places in England, even streets, particularly Tottenham Court Road and the names of friends whose addresses had been lost.

The most spectacular part of our journey, though, was the trip to Carrara, famous for its marble, to find the resistance hero, Alessandro. Frances accompa-nied me, and Bryan Morrison came with Joe. True enough, the first person we asked immediately pointed us in the direction of the Communist Party office above a small bookshop. Here there was an English speaking young man who acted as our interpreter and walked with us to a small tidy apartment, where Alessandro lived.

What does one expect when about to meet someone who has so clearly earned the accolade of hero? Perhaps a giant, fearsome and aggressive, arrogant and boasting, a man, full of himself? Alessandro was certainly none of these. He was rather diminutive, slim and sprightly, although well into his fifties. His face was lined and tanned. He looked and behaved like any of the men we had seen in Massa's town square becoming lachrymose over Mimi's final aria. Yet, as the day progressed and we toured the factory where the renowned Carrara marble was carved out of the mountain, cut and polished to be supplied to sculptors all over the world, we learned more about his life and his achievements.

His small company of local volunteers, consisting of communists, socialists and non-party anti-fascists had harassed the Italian fascist army even before the Germans became dominant in Liguria. Using the mountains for shelter and in particular the marble factory complex, they notched up many successes. It was however only when the Germans tried to move a large contingent of troops and equipment through the Bracco Pass towards Genoa that they had their major victory, killing, it was claimed, in the region of 300 Nazi soldiers. We also learned that Alessandro was the local doctor, more at home saving, than taking life.

For the children, however, the day's highlight was a ride in the funicular up the mountainside. Our stay in the area was one long delight; it was an incomparable experience and we savoured every moment.

We agreed that we would drive back together with the Morrisons as far as Genoa where they would return the way we had come; while we would travel back via Nice and up through France. This return journey, along the Italian and French Rivieras, we accomplished with more confidence, and we still had some money in hand as well as a greater knowledge of what we could do.

We had decided to dispense with camping and to take more time. We stopped at Alassio where we were baffled to find yellow posters and cards in the windows of several restaurants and shops as well as small hotels recommending Martin Rooks Travel. I assumed it was a British travel company, but there were few offering tours to Italy at that time.

Our return journey was neither as hazardous nor as difficult as we had anticipated and was much more enjoyable. Nice and Cannes lived up to our expectations, but with our limited resources we could only drive through and observe the high life of the moneyed classes with envy.

We arrived home tanned, exuberant and refreshed, but virtually penniless. We had been away for three weeks. There was not even enough left in the kitty to enable Lily to put together a proper meal. So, very early next morning I was obliged to work diligently on my cab, cleaning, polishing, making any necessary adjustments and touching up where required. I managed to get to the Carriage

The family at Expo 58, the World Fair in Brussels in 1958.

Office by 9.50am and was out sooner than I had thought possible looking for work. By early afternoon I had made enough money to buy food for the family.

That had been our first foreign travel experience, but by no means the last. We had now caught the bug, and considered ourselves experienced travellers. So, the following year we invited Lily's sister Rose with her husband Sam and their three boys to join us. I made a door for the open luggage side of the cab and put in a bench seat for two, next to me. Inside we made room for six, and with the entire luggage on the roof rack, we journeyed to the Adriatic and, later, again to the Italian Riviera. We made this voyage on three more occasions and each time it was a fresh and exhilarating experience.

During one such visit we stayed at the Hotel Ariani close to Rimini and through the children met a French family whose children were of similar ages to ours – the Chambauds from Amiens. They too were Jewish and through Lily, whose Yiddish was sufficient to make communication possible, we got to know them very well. Renée, the mother, was an attractive redhead who oozed warmth and tenderness and Moishe, her husband, was jovial and always had a smile. He was born in Poland and fled to France with his parents as a young boy. On the outbreak of war he joined the Free French Army and was at Dunkirk at the same time as I was. Evacuated to England, he soon joined General de Gaulle's Free French forces, and was selected to join a group sent back to Vichy France to help organise the resistance. He fought there with the Maquis.

They had with them three of their four children, and Frances became friends with their daughter Sylvie, and Michael with Serge, the elder of their two sons. We still remain friends after all these years.

On one occasion, we were travelling together with the Morrisons through Germany and decided to stop at Freiburg in the Black Forest. We found a typical German inn that could take us all for the night. We went down for dinner into a crowded room filled mostly with locals, and as the evening wore on the other guests become increasingly loud and raucous. A group began to sing recognisable Nazi songs with vigour, and seemingly addressed to us. We left early next morning, saddened to be met with such apparent hostility, but then we might have expected it. It was, after all, less than a decade since the end of the war and we were in southern Germany in what had once been a Nazi heartland.

CHAPTER SIXTEEN
Plunging into the real travel business

One day, following our return from our second trip abroad in 1956, and while visiting my old school friend, Joe and his wife, at their home in Loughton, we were discussing our adventures and we came to the conclusion that such foreign travel would soon become commonplace for many, not just the few, and we wanted to be part of it.

At Joe's suggestion we took the plunge and formed a company that, at his insistence, we called Riviera Holidays, since in his mind we would sell holidays only to the French Riviera, which he loved. I sold back a small insurance policy to raise the £100 I needed for my share in the enterprise, and we worked out a programme of rail holidays to Nice, Cannes and Mentone.

Our programme was based on similar holidays already being sold by other companies, but we had little idea of what it entailed. Joe wrote to hotels he personally selected from these brochures and received from each of them a leaflet describing its facilities but from most we received just a resort description. However each hotel included a price list from which he adduced our selling prices. Marketing consisted of a printed black and white A5 leaflet, which Lily and the children stuffed into envelopes and which I delivered after work, to social clubs, which were then an integral part of factory life. There was a vast network of these clubs, and all of them employed secretaries from whom I learned a great deal. Of course, I also canvassed the cab ranks while waiting for a job. We had no money for proper advertising, and my office consisted of a shared three-legged table in Joe's office, three floors above Barclays Bank on the corner of Calvert Avenue and Shoreditch High Street.

However, both of us slowly picked up the rudiments of the trade and began to understand what was involved if we were to achieve any success. By studying press articles on travel, I learned that the prime booking period for holidays was the three weeks immediately following Christmas. Advertising in the press started on the first Saturday after Christmas and the successful companies sold 95% of their summer holidays in that period, with the first Saturday providing a major part of the volume. I was extremely nervous about what we were doing but more particularly how we were going about it.

On that vital Saturday I was out in my cab at 4.30am and headed deliberately for Piccadilly in order to drive past the Skytours office. I was amazed; it was only just after 5 am, but already there was a queue of people stretching into Bolton Street and round the block and further, for almost a mile, waiting for the shop to open at 9 am. Excited, I drove down to Wilton Street by Victoria Station where I saw a similar group of people waiting for Martin Rooks to start taking bookings. Eventually I worked my way towards our office to find no queue, just one lady with a copy of our leaflet and a deposit. I dealt with the booking and then sat there all morning receiving neither a phone call nor a visit. And, into the bargain, I lost a valuable day's work!

It was a disaster. Our total bookings were in tens rather than the hundreds we'd dreamed about and too many were for single rooms and all in the high season. We were trying to sell holidays in resorts that our projected clientele could not aspire to, in hotel rooms we did not have, at much higher prices than the recognised, long established operators, and we lacked the minimal expertise and infrastructure to make it all work. I was, though, in retrospect, too harsh on myself. While I was well aware of Martin Rooks' history — his many years of transporting railway personnel and staff to holidays abroad, and the rise orf Skytours had been an even lengthier process.

In every walk of life there are myths and legends none more so than in travel. In an industry where growth was exponential and with vast changes in the industry's main structures the swift toppling of both long established companies and management coupled with the emergence of less contented, more aggressive and open-minded entrepreneurs made for the creation of icons. Sadly, one person whom I greatly admired for his vision and initiative never fully received the recognition due to him. Ted Langton's years in travel covered the last days of emigration through to the era of the modern air package holidays of which he was a major participant and innovator.

He became the archetypal buccaneering entrepreneur. Always an individualist his greatest characteristic was his inventiveness. This made him probably the most influential and innovative of all the 'pioneers' of the modern mass market travel operators.

Born before the turn of the century in a tiny seaside village between Liverpool and Preston, Langton left school as soon as was possible with the minimum education. His father was employed by the Vestey family who owned a wholesale butchers and Dewhursts, then a vast chain of retail butcher shops, all of which were backed by huge interests in Argentina. They introduced ships with freezing areas for the transport of carcases and were expanding rapidly. His father saw a future for him in the company and wanted him to join. But Langton had other ideas and made his way into the dock area of Liverpool, already at the peak of the shipping expansion and found a job with a shipping line primarily involved in Irish emigration to the United States.

Each morning he would travel on the first train from Southport to be in the office of the Galleon Shipping Line at 6.30am to meet the Irish passengers from Dublin and Belfast, when with colleagues he would issue onward tickets to the States and change monies. This lucrative business dropped off with the introduction of quotas by the American authorities and with almost immediate commencement of the 1914-18 war he joined the Merchant Navy.

In 1926 he opened a travel business in Birmingham in opposition to Poly Travel and George Lunn. All were close to the Cadbury factory and were greatly dependent on that organisation for business. He made his first venture into tour operating with a small programme of rail and coach holidays to Ostend, Paris and Lucerne which was not overly successful and was closed down following an invitation from King Alfonso of Spain to open a Spanish tourist office at 87 Regent Street in London's West End in 1927.

He claimed that his attachment to Spain was a consequence of an event during his boyhood. A Spanish ship ran aground off the coast of his village and a number of the sailors stayed on and created a colony within the village. He became fascinated by all that was Spanish and spent time learning the language and customs which served him well during his seafaring days.

The primary purpose of the office was to be the general agent for Transatlantica, a Spanish Shipping Line with one asset — The Reina Maria Christina, a former Union Castle ship. The ship was primarily used as a private yacht by the King. The office sold off the free dates for cruising.

He stayed there for four years during which he spent some time in Barcelona and Seville organising a number of ventures aimed at stimulating relations between Spain and Britain. He transported the whole company and props of the London show, *Wake Up and Dream,* starring Jessie Matthews and Sonnie Hale. The show ran for two weeks losing a considerable amount of money.

He approached the Football Association for the Corinthian F.C. to tour Spain and was refused but eventually he paid Bolton Wanderers £1000 to play one match in Barcelona and Jack Hylton and his orchestra did three sold out shows. His other responsibility was to visit travel agents throughout the UK, particularly Thomas Cook, who provided 60% of his trade.

The office closed with the collapse of the monarchy, and Langton returned to Southport to live with an aunt. He now had a wife and child. After one week he realised that Southport had no travel agency of any size and decided he would start one. However without an agency from one of the few major tour operators it would never get off the ground. He first approached George Lunn for his backing but although the latter didn't use agents, nevertheless he paved the way for him to become a Thomas Cook agent. However, this was never enough for Ted.

He had a friend with coaches who did day trips to Blackpool and Morecambe whom he approached to hire two coaches to him by the week. This was the beginning of his coach tour programme. One week holidays to Torquay, Bournemouth and Ilfracombe for £4, 19 shillings and sixpence, and to Newquay in Cornwall – nine days for £6, 19 shillings and sixpence.

He called his company Happiways Coach Tours, and in his second year he appointed almost any kind of business as agents, giving them 5% commission on their sales.. The company was an immediate success and in the following year he decided to start up holidays on the Continent.

Testing the water he rented a tiny kiosk in the Bedford Hotel in London and placed a single column classified advert in the *Daily Express* as Anglo-Continental Motorways. The response was overwhelming. For weeks the kiosk was bursting with mailbags. He later sold Happiways to Roberts of Rochdale for £5,000 and started a fresh operation. Blue Cars became his operating company, providing holidays in Ostend and Paris in its first year and in the following year further afield to the Rhine. It was successful enough for him to move his office to Shaftesbury Avenue in central London from where all his holidays now started. Travel was by train, boat to Brussels and onward by coach. In his first year operating to the Rhine he carried 3,000 passengers to Koblenz alone. His was the first low cost coach tour operation at that time.

With success came expansion. He purchased a Belgian coach company of the same name, 'Le Cars Bleu', and made a base at Ostend. Bought three specially built Land cruiser coaches and later three more Leylands and six Morris Commercials to further expand his programme. He then purchased or created associate companies in Milan and Paris and shared a sales office in New York with Frames Tours.

In 1936 he chartered four Rapide aircraft to fly from Lydd Airport in Kent to

1964 – Riviera Holidays is doing well and so are Spurs.

fly to Le Touquet, where he had based three coaches to take passengers to Brittany, the South of France and on to Spain.

At the outbreak of war in 1939, because of his travel knowledge, he was enlisted as captain in charge of the port of Manchester and also Liverpool dealing particularly with troop movements. All his travel operations closed down for the duration.

Immediately the war ended he unsuccessfully applied to be released from the navy to enable him to check on his companies. He was given authority to go to Ostend and make the contacts he needed to ascertain his position. In this he was reasonably successful, in that his contacts and many of his former employees were still in place, and in France he was able to recover almost all his fleet of coaches but he lost everything in Belgium and Italy.

He sold the Blue Cars operation to British Electric Traction in 1951. This did not include any of his other overseas operations which by now included Unitours which he owned jointly with Richard Day in New York and Leo Roupiez in Paris. This operation, formed just before the war, was aimed solely at the American

Riviera Sun, the company's promotional news sheet, August 1965.

market with Roupiez in charge of the European end and a separate company, Sovereign Tours, in London. Later a franchise was granted to Mike Alford in Los Angeles to sell in California. With the war ending, this in itself became a major operation with agents in all European and Middle Eastern countries.

Langton's sale to BET turned sour when he started Skytours a company providing air holidays to Europe almost immediately after the sale. BET's claim that Langton had used the Blue Cars' mailing list to kick start his new operation was upheld and he had to return £100,000.

The Skytours operation was in a different world. It was extremely difficult to set up a flight programme and put it on the market and sell. Charter air travel was tightly government controlled. You required a licence to fly anywhere. Licences were granted each year and applications had to be submitted months before the hearings to the Air Transport Licensing Board, whose main purpose appeared to be to safeguard the routes operated by BEA and BOAC. The licences would be applied for by the airline contracted by the operator and to overcome this major restriction, alternative airports were used in the applications. Perpignan for Barcelona, Alicante for Valencia and Rimini (a military airport) for the Adriatic. Small airports in Italy, Yugoslavia. and Austria, Belgium and France became important and grew accordingly, Similarly applicants had to avoid the major UK airports. Thus Croydon, Blackbushe, Luton, Gatwick, Southend and Stansted were pivotal to success.

With the granting of licences to new routes despite the objections of the national airlines, the licence holders would then object to any other airline operating what they considered their route, so there was the unedifying spectacle of airlines and operators donning different hats as they deemed opportune.

Those of us without sufficient means to employ barristers to fight our case usually came away empty handed. The alternative was to use foreign airlines which were more expensive and operated a reverse flight pattern which meant less time at resorts for our passengers, or one could try to purchase part capacity with a successful applicant, both of which raised the flying costs.

Langton who had set up an extensive programme for Skytours' opening in 1953 was caught on te horns of this dilemma and used many and various ways to get around the problem. He did obtain some licences to operate out of Blackbushe airport, which was in Berkshire some distance from London, and required a long coach journey. Few if any airlines would fly from such an isolated airport, so he teamed up with Jan Kozubski, an ex Polish army pilot, to fly a Dakota first of all out of Croydon airport and later from Blackbushe with their joint airline Independent Airlines. Kozubski's operations were questionable to say the least and he fell foul of the Board which took away the company's licence, only for Kozubski to repaint the craft the next day in a different livery, calling it Falcon Airways and repeating the operation later with Blue Sky. Several other nom de plumes enabled him to fly again and again. Eventually, Langton, recognising that his association with Kozubski would always keep him in conflict with the authorities, looked elsewhere for his air transport.

Langton, despite every effort, was unable to get a licence to fly to Palma in Majorca from any UK airport, but he realised he could fly to Maastricht in Holland, where he could touch down and then continue on to Palma. This he did successfully, operating as many flights as he wished out of Manston Airport.

He decided finally to look at the possibilities of operating his own airline and made contact, through Jed Williams a former BOAC pilot, and a consultant with EL Al, whom he understood was selling three of their Constellations which were, at the time, idle on the tarmac. Probably due to the growing number of passengers to Israel from the Unitours operation, he was given the aircraft, and EL AL agreed that they could be paid for over three years. This was the birth of Euravia. Euravia was later able to add five more Constellations obtained from Skyways, a long established operator now in decline. Later that year he had a substantial fleet which he based at Luton's fledgling airport, the first tour operator to do so. On May 5th 1962 the first Constellation took off with a plane load of Skytours' passengers from Manchester to Palma. In that year flights were operated from Birmingham, Manchester and of course Luton.

Aircraft costings were based on DOC (Direct Operational Costs) which only took weekend flying into consideration – from Friday mid-day to Sunday night. Weekends were the only times that the vast majority of package tour passengers could travel to cover their two weeks' holidays. The aircraft had very little flying to do mid-week.

Peter Sinclair, who owned a small company, Flightways, recognising the advantage of mid-week flying – low aircraft costs, no deposits or contract penalties (as I had with the Taxi Drivers' Benevolent Fund) – set up an operation of 10 and 11 day holidays flying into Madrid and onward by coach to Malaga or Tangier, both relatively unknown destinations at that time. It failed miserably. Langton recognised that the idea was sound but the destinations were not and the coach journey was too long. The prices were too high. In the following year he set up a programme of 11 and 12 day holidays to the Costa Brava which proved to be tremendously popular and were over-subscribed. He expanded the principle to Majorca and other resorts making fullest use of his aircraft, which in turn allowed him to reduce weekend prices where needed but most importantly, increased profits. Of course, mid-week shorter-stay holidays were taken up by other operators until it became established practice in the business.

The exponential growth of Skytours meant that the Constellations were soon too small for many of the airline's routes and it became necessary to find replacements. BOAC had ended the use of their Britannia 102 fleet of six aircraft and had mothballed them at Cambridge. Euravia purchased a number of these in 1964 and changed the name to Britannia Airways. By the summer of 1965 there were five in operation in addition to the Constellations. Langton had finally rid himself of the Kozubski problem.

This increase of tourists from the UK and the growth of tourism in other European countries put considerable pressure on hotels, particularly in Spain and the Balearics. Attempting to alleviate this problem he built a totally new hotel in Majorca, the Arenal Park in Arenal, and invested heavily in the 900 bed Hotel Taurus Park on the Costa Brava. Because the latter was in an isolated position, he included nightly entertainment in the price and employed his own management team to control meals and other amenities. He claimed the Taurus Park helped to distinguish Skytours from other operators by establishing a new concept. He had learned a great deal from his earlier ownership of a much smaller property in Playa San Juan on the Costa Brava, which had set the standard and price value for the Skytours operation.

He was the first into Benidorm using the Avenida Palace, The Bristol and the

Almudaina in the village. These remained popular despite the ribbon growth of hotels along the beaches.

He always endeavoured to have exclusivity at the hotels he used. This gave him freedom to price his holidays without fear of being undercut by other operators who nevertheless continuously tried to obtain a minimal number of rooms even if at a much higher price, which could then be sold at prices below Skytours to indicate that their holidays were cheaper.

Finding hotel beds in the popular resorts was a constant problem for all tour operators not just from the UK. Langton had the advantage of having contracts which year after year he fulfilled and his hoteliers were happy to stay with him. Success breeds success. He gained an early foothold in Calamillor and Cala Bona and was the first to fly into Tenerife in the Canary Islands, Klagenfurt in Austria and Ljubljana in Yugoslavia. He operated flights from several provincial UK airports.

In April 1965 he sold Skytours and Britannia Airways lock, stock and barrel to the Thomson Organisation. Riviera was purchased by Thomson at exactly the same time. It was shortly after this that I first met Langton, of whom I had heard so much. In his time he had owned The George Hotel in Colchester, Barkers Club and Winstons in London. Although not a gambler he owned a stable with a string of horses.

I found Ted Langton to be a complex man. So did the Thomson hierarchy, for whom he actively displayed contempt, and from the very early days was not very cooperative. His last venture was to resuscitate a cruise programme which I had aborted when I had control at Thomsons. He hired the Queen Frederica from the Chandris line and set up a programme of Sovereign back-to-back holidays. but it failed.

He retired to the Island of Majorca, where unable to resist hotel involvement, he bought the small hotel Morocco in Palma Nova where he could be found most days, with his dog Zeke, drinking steadily at the bar. He died peacefully but suddenly a few years later.

CHAPTER SEVENTEEN
Riviera takes off

My own early efforts at selling our product were through the clubs and on the cab ranks as I worked. I also realised, somewhat late in the day, that club secretaries were not interested in individual bookings; they concentrated on group activities for whatever event or function they took on. Paris at Easter, for example, was fast becoming an event. This followed the hundreds of football teams that had travelled to France and Belgium to play games arranged for them and who were transported mainly by coach via Ostend.

My very first football booking was for 36 players from Bedford Kempsford Rovers to fly from Luton for the week-end. They had arranged their own accommodation and matches and just needed someone to arrange their flight. There were literally hundreds of airlines at that time, but 'airline' is perhaps a rather inflated term. Most consisted of one old DC3 or Viking usually owned by an ex-RAF pilot trying to make it in the fast expanding aviation business.

Easter was their busiest time and I had to make numerous calls until I was finally successful in securing a DC3 based in Birmingham, which I booked to fly from Luton to Paris on the Thursday, to stay over and return on the following Monday evening.

Luton then consisted of a single hangar with minimum facilities and no staff. Joe Morrison with his son Bryan, my son Michael and I issued the tickets, loaded the luggage and passengers and saw the plane off. This was our very first flight venture, on which we made very little money, but nevertheless we were in business.

I had one other success at the time. I obtained a booking for 53 people from Sainsbury's sausage factory, then based in Stamford Street, to Paris at Easter the following year. This time it was a complete package and included accommodation. Near the time, Joe and I flew by BEA to Paris but had an arduous and difficult time finding a hotel prepared to take the group. We almost took one, only to learn from a local restaurateur that it was a brothel. But, after a sleepless night, we were eventually successful. We bought group travel tickets from Alex Homatas of Cyprus Travel. He was a charming and helpful Greek Cypriot who specialised in holidays for his community. We were also helped by Bill Richards, his general manager, who went out of his way to be of assistance. Joe also knew of a party comrade, Dave Wallis, who was a teacher of French and a budding author, who agreed to travel as courier, and with his agreement we tied it up.

All was successful and our clients had a good time despite being forced, at one point, to line up against a wall by machine-gun-toting gendarmes who thought they might be Algerian saboteurs. It was the time of the Algerian uprising against French occupation of their country and the police were edgy.

Such were the minor irritants we had to deal with. I could, though, not envisage cancelling our ambitious programme, which would certainly have been the easier thing to do. Joe, ever the optimist, confidently thought we should go ahead as we had planned and travel to the south of France to arrange the hotels. He was happy to go with his wife Di and thought it unnecessary for me to go with him; the compromise was that we all went. Flying all the way was too expensive, so we flew to Paris and then onward by train. We had very little money, but this did not bother Joe, he had it all worked out – the hotels would be so happy to see us that they would bend over backwards providing us not only with food but also rooms.

I had great difficulty persuading Lily to fly. Following my own flight to Paris, I enthused about flying and in particular landing at Heathrow in the dark. Despite all my enthusiasm, though, she remained extremely nervous, and it required two stiff brandies in the departure lounge to calm her.

We took off in a BEA Viscount and all was well until we became aware of some disconcerting activity among the stewards, shortly followed by a message from the captain announcing that there was a technical problem and we had to return to Heathrow. Until we actually landed, we would have to circle around for some considerable time to use up surplus fuel.

It took several more brandies and considerable persuasion to get Lily on to the plane again. The onward journey from Paris by rail was fine but we found the hoteliers were completely and utterly uninterested in our project. This was most distressing. After unsuccessful visits to eleven or more by early afternoon, we were tired, hungry and became ever more despondent. Our final call in Nice was the Hotel Impèriale, a smart establishment, and our request to see the manager, brought forth a young genial Corsican who we discovered was also the proprietor. Following some discussion, he astonishingly invited us to lunch and provided a full five-course French meal with wines all of a very high standard and agreed to take our miserable few bookings.

Leaving refreshed and uplifted, I persuaded Joe to travel with me into Italy and look for future resorts and hotels. We took a bus, which stopped at every major and minor resort and village as far as Alassio, where, arriving late in the day, tired and dishevelled, we found the town very quiet, with closed shops and few people. Asking for a hotel we were pointed in the direction of the Pensione Toscana. The pensione consisted of a large restaurant with a kitchen visible through a glass wall and one floor of newly built rooms all with baths and showers en suite. We explained who we were and what we were doing on the Italian Riviera in early February but it made little impact. We decided to make the best of the situation and after putting our baggage in our allotted rooms, we went to eat. The restaurant fare was sumptuous with a Maitre d' who we learned later was the eldest son of the family Mantellessi who owned and managed the establishment. It was obvious, though, that the person who made it all function was Signora Beppa. Our limited acquaintance with Italian food was that supplied in the Spaghetti House on the corner of Goodge Street, which we frequented as often as we could afford to do. To have two such wonderful culinary experiences in one day was beyond our wildest dreams, and more than that, it bolstered my desire to make it work. The Signora, as she was known, was a tiny lady who sat throughout meal times on a high stool from which she could oversee everything coming out of the kitchen. She also had a full view of the restaurant, enabling her to ensure that the service was immaculate. This hotel later became our flagship and, as our business grew, so did the reputation of the hotel, which seemed to build an additional floor in every off-season. We later learned that the family had purchased a farm in Tuscany which provided most of the ingredients used in the kitchen including its fine wine.

The morning after that first visit, we took a stroll around the town. We saw small cardboard posters in shops, pensions and cafés announcing that Martin Rooks used or recommended them. This was the same Martin Rooks whose office I had seen besieged by long queues, and envied on that first booking day. Peter Rooks who owned the company had been a railwayman and his was one of the many small companies, as well as individuals, who took advantage of the reciprocal facility enjoyed by British Rail workers to travel cheaply on European railways by providing transfers and accommodation. He had since successfully progressed into the wider tour-operating business. This knowledge further convinced me that choosing the French Riviera had been a terrible mistake and that if we were to stay in business we had to concentrate on Italy.

Our stay at the Toscana had bitten deeply into our finances and when we stopped at Monte Carlo on the return journey we realised we didn't have enough even to cover a room for the night. On the philosophy of shit or bust, we went to the casino were I was nominated to play. Once I won some money, Joe collected it until we had enough to get us a bed for the night. Perhaps I really was the son of my father!!

On the return rail journey to Paris we were obliged to survive on bread and cheese. When we reached Paris it was snowing heavily and, as we joined the queue for the return flight, we heard the terrible news of the air crash at Munich airport in which eight of Manchester United's best players were killed and many others badly injured. As a result, Matt Busby, their manager, was forced to field his third team in future games.

We were unsure whether our plane would take off under the circumstances. It was an anxious time since we knew that once a passenger had checked in for a flight they automatically became the responsibility of the airline. If you had not yet passed through you were on your own. We were in the latter category and the thought of spending the night on an airport bench was not a pleasant one. With great difficulty and endless argument we managed to get BEA to lend us £5 each to see us through.

By the end of that holiday season we were more than broke − in the region of £200 in debt. It was then that Joe decided, because of his accountancy business, he could not continue in travel because of the danger that his own company would go bust as a result. It was clear, if I wished to carry on, I was on my own. He did not surrender his shares, but was no longer a director, nor was he directly involved anymore.

I had a dilemma: I had no money, and neither could I get support from a bank, and even if I could find someone to purchase Joe's shares, it was doubtful whether he would sell. I also had no premises to work from. But I'd already learned a lot about the travel industry, enough to recognise both the turbulence, the pitfalls, but also the potential. I had to admit that tour operating was not possible for me at that time, so decided to become a travel agent selling other tour operators' holidays. To my cabbie colleagues, interested acquaintances and all those with whom I came in contact, I was someone with a special knowledge to whom they could talk. I became available at any reasonable time, night and day and any place.

My sister Rita, who had a small house in St. Ann's Road in Tottenham kindly allowed me to use her front room as an office. This gave me an address, enabling me to receive brochures from tour operators, but i couldn't use it as a sales point. My main and only possible way to move forward was to continue with the social clubs and extend sales to my fellow cab drivers and others.

1959 turned out to be a good year. There were a number of contributory factors, not least, with Joe out of the way I could now make my own decisions. I also felt easier about feeding off those with greater or more recent experiences. I made it my business to talk to anyone who'd been abroad and this was invaluable. That year I sold a sufficient number of package tours and, by dint of hard work, managed to clear all the accumulated debts. But, most importantly, I also had several groups booked for the following year, 1960.

Two coach loads from Waterlows', the printers' social club to Zell am See in Austria was a substantial coup, but of even greater significance, I made an arrangement with the Taxi Drivers' Benevolent Fund to provide a series of holidays by air to the Toscana Hotel in Alassio with Viking flights to Nice and coach transfers to the resort, and with departures every Monday from June until September. This was a tremendous undertaking, but a great opportunity. I had a number of meetings with Bernie Fogelman, the fund's treasurer and secretary. All financial obligations were down to me, as was advertising and licensing.

Tour operations by air were subject to draconian regulations. The primary object of the Air Transport Licensing Board was to protect our national airlines – BEA and BOAC – and it was difficult, in fact virtually impossible, to obtain a licence to operate independent flights on their routes. . The restrictions operating to prevent or at least discourage 'new flying' could be overcome if a 'group of like-minded people' was involved, and the 'Fund' was such a group. Many artificial groups were formed at the time specifically to overcome these restrictions – like bird fanciers or wine tasters and, in the major league, 'The family and friends'. Using this tactic it was possible to fly across the Atlantic and to Australia at affordable prices. Mine, though, was a genuine group. I chose Monday departures because practically all chartered air holiday departures were on weekends – starting on Friday evening and finishing on Sunday night or very early on Monday mornings – and I could get a good deal by travelling outside these times; taxi drivers were not restricted by working weeks as most employees were.

To facilitate my idea I arranged a meeting with Overseas Aviation who had offices above a restaurant in Panton Street. Overseas, an established airline, had introduced BOAC Canadair Argonauts into its extensive operations which included transporting Dutch and German holidaymakers to European holiday resorts, as well as an established programme with British operators and a number of scheduled air routes.

I was apprehensive as I left my cab opposite Angelo's and, dressed impeccably, I walked to the offices to find two smart young men, in identical coloured waistcoats, fashionable at that time, waiting for me at the door. John Hughes and Mike Kemp took me to the Comedy restaurant below the offices and over the meal we agreed a contract which was quite innocuous for me since I had no obligation to fly, no deposit to pay and no penalties whatsoever. They gave a commitment to fly; all I had to do was find the passengers! The price was pretty good and I came away well fed and very pleased with myself.

Later in the week, when walking up Stamford Hill on the way to the Regent cinema with my family, it suddenly dawned on me the enormity of the task I had set myself and I suddenly froze to a block of ice. Joe, I suppose, realising the potential was still there and with the danger of collapse now receded, decided to become active in the company once again. I was of two minds about it, but with little that I could do to stop him, and still believing in his business experience, I agreed.

In the event all trips with my groups were successful but there were difficulties with the taxi group. I had a good number of people booked, but they were spread all over the series. Ideally, I needed 90%, but at least 80% passenger load, but fell far short of that. Joe had a client who was a friend of Vladimir Raitz, the MD and proprietor of Horizon Holidays, and Joe approached him about the problem. To our surprise, we discovered that he was in similar difficulties with his programme to the Italian Riviera. He had a licensed series to Turin from whence there was a long drive to his hotels along the coast, so he welcomed my numbers. It was a good deal for my passengers, since the flights were by BKS Viscounts and on the transfers they were provided with dinner at one of the superior hotels Horizon used. The flights were also on the weekend, which enabled me to satisfy those for whom the day of flying was important. Best of all, his package included not only the flights but also the transfers and the meal en route. Even then the cost to me was one pound less than my flight cost alone would have been and without the costly transfer along the coast from Nice airport. All of this made the series very profitable. On 1st December 1960, on the basis of the successes of that year and the prospects for the following, I gave up 'cabbing' and plunged full time into travel.

CHAPTER EIGHTEEN
Expanding into air travel

I found myself in an exciting and adventurous world. There was a growing recognition by the general public of the advantages of holidaying in the sun and they yearned for it. That remained the major travel incentive, although many of those who had fought in Italy, France and even further afield were also keen to return for nostalgic reasons. There were others who saw in this desire a rosy future for the providers, the tour operators and travel agents whose numbers exploded exponentially.

Just as the introduction of steam trains and ships had expanded emigration travel, so the 1939-45 war speeded and expanded the use of aircraft and, with the end of the war, there was an abundance of mothballed planes available for purchase and pilots to fly them. It was estimated that in the first decade after the war there were in excess of 350 individual companies formed to operate or maintain aircraft in the UK alone. Not all survived, but several raced ahead, reaping the benefits of the Berlin Blockade and the need to break it, as well as a number of national strikes, where aircraft were used extensively to overcome transport difficulties. For the majority of these, however, there was oblivion

This was also true of agents and tour operators. There were of course the established travel agents, but there were also the part timers who had until then sold coach tours as a source of extra revenue. Now, many firms transferred their businesses from tobacconists and cobblers into full-time travel agencies. These, despite artificial restrictions engineered against them by the incumbents, found air holidays to sell from the new operators, who were themselves fighting against the same contrived restrictions.

The Creative Travel Agents Consortium was formed as a consequence of the great depression of the 1930s which hit the travel industry dramatically. Travel abroad was thought by many to be unpatriotic and more and more agencies were closing as a result of the price war that followed the crisis. 'The railways had never been co-operative and had always grudged us their meagre concessions. Now this traffic dwindled alarmingly. They took the initiative and tried to prevent further bankruptcies. We were ruining ourselves with our rivalry. In the jargon of the politicians we had to stand together so the Southern Railways called a truce' (*The Holiday Story* by R.G. Studd). Its members were Cooks, Dean & Dawson, Hickie Borman, Grant & Co, Wayfarers Travel Association, Polytechnic Travel Association, The Workers Travel Association, Sir Henry Lunn, Pickfords and Frames, all of whom decided that while keeping their independence they would agree the selling price of all tours. The CTAC at that time was purely restrictive, it was there to ensure that price cutting was limited. It was not possible for a new comer to become a member of this consortium.

Later it changed into something more aggressive, but the introduction of low cost air travel became its nemesis. Yet in its early days Poly had been progressive in ideas. It had introduced Belgium as a holiday resort for British travellers. In 1924 a ten day holiday in Ostend and or Blankenberge cost £4, 16 shillings and sixpence. From here there were excursions by coach into Holland. They invented the courier by having a uniformed army of trained representatives at stations and resorts who were easily distinguishable by their specially designed cap with a white band and seagull logo.

It was Poly that sent the first British holidaymakers by air when a four-engined Hercules aircraft with 24 passengers took off from Croydon Airport and was the first large plane to land at Basle Airport. The series was a success with nearly a thousand passengers a year travelling to the Continent by air. Among them was my aunt Stella who was persuaded to travel as matron to a group of pupils from Uppingham School. In 1933 Poly announced a 14 day air cruise to seven European capitals. These included Amsterdam, Berlin, Vienna, Budapest, Rome, Marseilles and Paris.

It was around this time that Dean and Dawson introduced a 25 guinea train cruise of Austria and Hungary. Disaster was predicted but even though the cruise was introduced towards the end of the season, thousands booked according to Commander Studd of Lunn Poly.

There were other irritants among the manyf new entrepreneurs with fresh ideas. One such was Joseph Gatti, an asylum seeker who came to Britain from Mussolini's fascist Italy. He had been an active trade unionist in the Adriatic region of Italy and left in 1938 by working on a boat collecting coal from Swansea from where he jumped ship to work in the kitchens of various restaurants. With the outbreak of war he, along with thousands of Italians and others, was interned as an 'enemy alien'.

At the end of the war he renwed contact with his family. His elder brother was now a Communist leader in one of the major trade unions on the Adriatic. From the end of the war trade unions took up the plight of the many small to medium-sized boarding houses (pensions) that were empty in the towns that were devoid of visitors. Gatti soon caught on to this new phenomena of overseas travel and persuaded his brother that there might be some possibilities for his region. Between them they devised an agreement that made a number of the best pensions available in a programme that Gatti would set up in Britain. Gatti, with the assistance of a bright young couple of Italians, Anna and Umberto Cassa, and positive help received through his Labour and trade union connections in the UK, set up Intertours. He then had to battle British Rail, but again his union and parliamentary connections eased his way, and in 1958 a train load of mostly young people went each Saturday over 16 weeks on 15 day holidays to Rimini. These included three meals each day and transfers at a cost of only 28 guineas. This opened up the hitherto unknown Adriatic coast. Intertours continued to be successful for four more years until the expansion of air holidays. Gatti refused to believe that rail holidays of the kind he provided could be superseded by air travel. He found the required flying contracts too complicated and the risk element too great, and above all, found employing people who could assist him too expensive. It was his conservative attitude that rapidly destroyed his business. His was just another example in the long history of the travel industry of failure to accept and adapt to new ideas proving fatal. The combination that destroyed Intertours also progressively ended the edifice that was the CATC.

Martin Rooks whose posters spread around Alassio I had found so intriguing did recognise the way forward. Peter Rooks was a railwayman who started to provide hotel accommodation at resorts in Italy soon after the war ended to British railway workers, all of whom had access to free rail travel on European railways. The company grew steadily, but unlike Gatti, Peter recognised where the future lay and changed over to air packages with a small but popular programme open to the general public. It was an overwhelming success and Rooks' Holidays were completely sold out in the two weeks after Christmas. The queues at their offices in Wilton Street adjacent to Victoria Station on the first Saturday required police controls. After Peter's death the company was taken over by Owners Abroad who in turn became First Choice.

The members of CTAC were also the instigators of the Association of British

Travel Agents (ABTA). The idea of ABTA was dreamed up by the hierarchy at Cooks with the much admired Jimmy Maxwell as its chief protagonist. In its requirements for membership an applicant was required to have both a British Rail and BEA licence. Since it was extremely difficult to obtain either of these the membership remained small and exclusive.

The growing number of tour operators outside ABTA supplied the expanding numbers of non-ABTA agents with sufficient holidays and vice versa, that ABTA members lost out on the rapid industry growth. Soon the idea of creating a separate trade organisation was mooted and then formed by Gerald Don of Don Tours and an associate named Potter. This added to the pressure on ABTA which itself had been formed only a few years earlier. However the major factor in the downfall of many of the old stalwarts was their inability to see and to accept the changes taking place around them. I was pleased to note in my second year of operation, being alluded to by R. R. May, the chairman of Lunns, at the company's annual dinner as: 'the cab driver who assumes he knows how to organise travel better than us'. Eventually finding itself seriously challenged, the ABTA establishment agreed to drop the barriers they had established to maintain their oligarchy. In 1965 under the guidance of 'Tubby' Garner and 'Hoppy' Hopkinson 'Operation Stabiliser' took place and with membership rules relaxed and entry made easier, ABTA membership exploded.

In 1961 Riviera expanded its core business, offering low cost air package holidays. Now that I was full time I was able to do the work essential for growth. We began to move on from group travel to selling individual family holidays. However, one of our last groups gave the impetus to move ahead in several directions. In 1960 I booked a group of 54 members of the sports club of Smith's Meters in Croydon, South London for a holiday on the Italian Adriatic coast for the following year. Considering the impact that Intertours had made, I considered it imperative that we should be active in Italy and more specifically on the Adriatic. First I had to find an agent, which I did through the Italian Tourist Board, and then make the choice from a number on offer. My choice of company, Viaggi Condor, was made simply because it had a representative, a Mrs. O'Hara, living in Scotland, and therefore easy to reach. It was from her that I gathered that it was her father who ran the agency based in Rimini.

I flew via Milan in late September and met Signor Martelli. I gathered that his company had been formed with assistance from, if not on behalf of, the PSD, the Italian Social Democratic Party. In this new Italy it appeared that political parties realised it was important to promote tourism. Martelli was a quiet, gentle man and we got along very well. Subsequently, as tourism in Emillio Romagna developed, he was toppled and the company taken over by a brash, younger man.

Promoting Riviera on London buses in the sixties.

The next day we visited a number of hotels and pensions in Rimini. I had this firm group I could offer and felt confident this would be an inducement. Unfortunately it was for the first two weeks of August, part of Ferrogusta, the main Italian annual holiday period, when all the major cities closed down. Ferrogusta also included the last two weeks of July. At his suggestion we moved on to a nearby, tiny, and as yet undeveloped resort, Cattolica. It had a desolate appearance when I looked it over, since everywhere was closed for the holidays. It consisted of a row of ageing hotels, directly on the narrow beach from which led streets containing a varied selection of pensions, and further back other pensions above shops situated directly on secondary roads.

The proprietor of the Hotel Luxor, a Snr. Signorini appeared to be a man of substance and he agreed without coercion to accept my group in his hotel on the dates required. I later learned that it was common knowledge that the same Signorini had close associations with the Mafia, but I was never pressured by any of his dubious acquaintances. Without prompting, he suggested that I would need another good pension and personally took me to see Maria at the Pension Puppi (little doll guest house). I was immediately impressed by Maria, a young woman, with a baby in a high chair who she was feeding, an activity which ceased only when the baby gave up. She spoke good English and was sparky. Her Zia (auntie) was the cook and she was excellent. I felt that this was a winner and signed a contract for most of the 40 rooms in the building. The next day I was taken to see the almost completed Hotel Senior, adjacent to the Puppi and Hotel Windsor, and at each I contracted rooms. These were without doubt the best contracts I ever made for they were the basis for our future success. Finally I took a few beds at the posh

Hotel Astoria on the beach, owned by two brothers, Franco and Sandro Gabbellini.

This was the start of a long business association during which time many solid friendships were created and sustained. The Hotel Senior too was family owned and managed by Inez, a deeply religious, charming, yet resolute, but welcoming lady. Andrew, her husband, was a school teacher seen only after school hours, but very involved in the welfare of his pupils and the community. If not a communist, he was certainly a very committed socialist. His participation in the hotel management, however, appeared to be minimal. The other part owner was Mario, the brother of Inez. He was the local mayor and a tough communist. Somewhat distrustful of me, despite my credentials, he was very much aware of the pitfalls of business and the need to exercise controls. We all became great friends and I was often called upon to advise and was very willing to do so. It was of great assistance to me in that I learned a lot about hotel management at that level.

With hotels and pensions booked in Cattolica, all I needed was something in Rimini, the largest of all the resorts along the coast, to finalise my programme. Snr. Martelli suggested the Pension Mimosa. Unfortunately he was unable to accompany me, so I introduced myself in my stumbling Italian to Doctor Giorgio, who was enjoying a late lunch. He insisted that I join him, which I did. I had already a slight acquaintance with garlic but never as overpowering as in that meal. My breath could be sniffed a mile off! Nevertheless expressing much delight at the meal, which had been prepared by his mother, I obtained a number of rooms and set out to my own hotel in Rimini – The Palace.

I noticed that Visconti's film *Rocco and his Brothers* was showing in the local cinema and decided to see it, but I was so ill after that meal, that I couldn't manage it. I purchased various cures in the local chemist and went to bed swearing to check that the meals provided for our clients would not be so aggressive. Garlic, particularly at that time, was not exactly a favoured British ingredient.

We sold the pension extremely well and received excellent reports, so when holidaying with my family nearby, I felt compelled to call on Giorgio. He was most welcoming and extremely pleased with our bookings and demanded that I come with my family for lunch on the following Friday. Registering my reluctance, he thought, correctly, it must be to do with the food, but he assumed that I objected to fish which was the main course that day and said he would provide me with something different. He refused to take no for an answer, and we soon found ourselves in the restaurant eating lunch. It was excellent, as were the meals eaten by my clients, and I felt guilty that I had spoken so disparagingly about his cuisine. I said so to Lily, who had always thought I was exaggerating. Near the end of the meal Giorgio bent over to ask if I was satisfied. The garlic odour from his mouth was overpowering and recalled that other most unfortunate lunch.

CHAPTER NINETEEN
Spurs air lift – it's a record

"More than 2,500 Spurs fans will fly to Rotterdam for the Spurs' Game on Wednesday – the biggest air-lift in British sporting history.

The Spurs Supporters' Club have commandeered sixty-five coaches to take them to Gatwick, Southend or Luton where they will fill thirty-three planes bound for Rotterdam.

Man behind the massive air-lift, Aubrey Morris, travel chief and member of Spurs Supporters' Club, said last night "We have had to turn down nearly 2,000 applicants including a great number of youngsters."

Morris said he had been astonished by the rush for seats.

"Only two coach loads went to Maine Road on Saturday and it just shows that fans are growing more and more conscious of travelling by air to big games abroad.

Judging from the flood of applications for passports more than half of the fans going to Rotterdam will be travelling abroad for the first time."

Alan Williams *(Daily Express)*

In the early hours of Saturday March 4th 1961 I drove to Gatwick Airport with my son Michael and two long time supporters of Tottenham Hotspur Football Club. We were about to fly on the first ever air charter for soccer fans. My companions were unaware of my concerns, in particular whether the aircraft I had chartered, a Viscount of Maitland Drewery Aviation, would be ready to fly. As we drove into the airport we could see the aircraft on the tarmac and I felt more comfortable. This was to be the start of Riviera Holidays' adventure into European football with the fabulous Spurs and the glory, glory days.

Ever anxious to expand, and flushed with the success of the taxi drivers' charter holidays, I met a friend of mine, Sidney Silver, after a Spurs' game and, as serious supporters, we came up with the idea of arranging something similar in conjunction with the supporters club. Soon after, we got together with the treasurer, Hymie Lewis, and Secretary, Eddie Edwards, to discuss the idea. They were not prepared to come on board, it was obviously too big a thing for them to handle. The supporters club concentrated on coaching spectators to away games, but the idea we were suggesting was beyond their horizons. Hymie Lewis was possibly more open, and maybe it was his wartime experiences in the army that made him more receptive. He spoke very little and appeared to be a very doleful character. It was only later that I learned that when he returned home on compassionate leave just days before the end of the war, because his wife had given birth to their first child, he walked into the desolation and destruction of his home and the loss of his wife and baby. That experience had left a deep scar. The very last Nazi missile of the war had demolished Hughes Mansions where he lived in London's East End on the very day he returned home.

When the draw for the sixth round of the FA Cup was announced and Spurs were drawn away to play Sunderland, I thought I would try and fill an aircraft to fly from Gatwick to Newcastle and then take fans on to the game by coach. I arranged the flight of a Viscount with 74 seats with Maitland Drewery, through Peter Dorrington, and distributed leaflets at the first home game. The total cost was £12 and 10 shillings. A few days before departure I had a meeting with Dorrington and told him that as I only had 47 passengers it was unlikely that we could proceed. Eventually we made a deal and the flight was on, even though I knew that we would not make a penny, and possibly lose on it. However having paid the cash I then became more concerned that if the airline was in trouble, as it appeared, and went into liquidation, we would be going nowhere and have nothing to show for our effort. However, Dorrington kept to the deal and the flight did go but the plane returned only to be impounded immediately on landing back at its base.

It had been a great day with more than 61,000 spectators, most of whom were roaring for the home side to win. We found ourselves in the midst of what must have been the most fanatical of the Sunderland supporters. Tottenham took the lead after nine minutes and played at their best, but the second half was a transformation. The crowd reached a frenzy, urging Sunderland forward and they had corner after corner until McPhail scored the equaliser. Then there was a pitch invasion, and we seriously feared for our lives. We were like aliens surrounded by hoards of abusive and aggressive natives. My pleasant memories with my war-time Geordie mates were wiped away, and for the rest of the game my concern was for the safety of my group and, in particular, my son Michael and another young lad.

Danny Blanchflower, the Spurs' captain, later wrote 'Nothing I have ever heard equalled the intensity of that wild roar when Sunderland drew level with Spurs in that sixth round tie.' It was reported that in the delay caused by the crowd eruption, Blanchflower spoke to each and every Spurs player to calm them down and give new instructions. It clearly worked, for from then on, whatever Sunderland threw at them the Spurs players held firm. The game ended a 1-1 draw. We also came away in one piece, our spirits high and our hearts filled with joy. The following Wednesday, Spurs won the replay by five goals to nil, and went on to win the FA Cup and do the double, the first team to manage that since Aston Villa in 1897. In a small but significant way we had now established our-selves, at least in our own minds, as the 'official' Spurs travel club, and Spurs would soon be playing in the European Cup competition with home and away games in each round except the final!

In the preliminary round of the competition Spurs were drawn away to Górnik Zabrze in Poland, the game to be played on September 13th 1961. I persuaded Joe and Sidney that we should have a shot at this. It had never been attempted before and we had a great deal of trepidation. Besides, our bread and butter tour programme was expanding and this project could take away valuable resources.

I made contact with a young sales rep at British Eagle, Mike Prior, who as a keen football fan showed great interest in the idea. We made a deal for one Britannia aircraft to do a day trip to Poland. Once again the supporters' club would not sponsor or assist us and we were on our own. Without the means of advertising, we enrolled everyone we could. At each and every home game and the occasional away match Sid and I with the whole family distributed leaflets. In the end, we managed to fill the aircraft with enthusiastic supporters and, despite the weather, the trip was a huge success. But not for Spurs, who lost by four goals to three after they had been four goals down. The return game played one week later in front of more than 60,000, mostly Spurs fans, was won by Tottenham — eight goals to nil!

In the subsequent first round Tottenham played Feijenoord in Rotterdam and again we sent a plane-load of spectators. Spurs won the away game, drew at home and went on to play Dukla, the Czech champions, in the quarter finals in Prague. We had to turn people away after two British Eagle Britannia aircraft were filled to the brim. Tottenham lost that game one nil and to add to the misery we encoun-tered currency difficulties at the airport before leaving. We were given to under-

With Spurs fans in Lisbon for the game against Benfica in 1963.

stand that Czech money was the only currency that could be used in the country. The local currency was exchanged when we arrived and that in itself was not easy. Each individual had to purchase local currency to spend while in the country and was given a receipt which he had to keep in order to change back again whatever they had left into Sterling. No one could leave the country with local currency. The theory was to prevent a black market in foreign currency operating.

I was absolutely astounded when we arrived back at the airport late at night, after a miserable day to find it deserted except for our two aircraft on the tarmac ready to go. There was no one able or prepared to change the currency and the people handling the aircraft's departure were unable to help. The wrangling and demonstrable lack of interest was most disheartening. The pilots were going to take off without us unless we agreed to pay £100 per aircraft per hour in demurrage. This was frustrating for the passengers but it was devastating for us. Having to pay that kind of money would have been an absolute disaster. Eventually, to overcome the problem, we collected the individual currencies ourselves noting the amount taken from each of the passengers which we left with a sympathetic Czech airline official and promised our travellers that we would deal with the problem. The very next day I went to the Czech embassy, harangued various officials, got the exchange sorted out and returned monies to those who had been affected.

Spurs' opponent in the semi-final was Benfica, the cup holders, who were at their peak under their Hungarian coach, Bela Guttman, who had put together a team of Portuguese and Mozambiquan players, including the very young Eusebio.

We had a little more time to prepare for this venture and put together a one-day trip – also two nights with hotel accommodation, as well as a three and five nights package, travelling by ferry from Southampton to Lisbon and return. This was our greatest challenge and required travelling to Lisbon to check hotels, transfers and excursions beforehand. We took the opportunity to explore Lisbon. The weather was gorgeous and we would sit down to a meal at 10 or 11 in the evening in splendid restaurants. I recall this was the first time I was able to choose live lobster, from a tank in the centre of the restaurant.

Surprisingly, all went well with our arrangements. Our passengers were not sophisticated travellers and had to be guided more than we might have hoped, yet only one person went astray. The game was played under floodlights on a beautiful balmy evening. The large Benfica stadium was full and our relatively tiny contingent had to work hard to be heard at all.

Spurs went two down very quickly and, despite Bobby Smith pulling one back, Benfica won by three goals to one. There was a great deal of controversy over apparently good Spurs' goals being disallowed by the Swiss referee. Spurs were beaten, but the disappointment was ameliorated by having watched a first class game and experiencing a magnificent trip. By far the majority of those who travelled with us had never before experienced the wonderful warmth of southern climes. For the first time in the competition Spurs failed to reverse the situation in the home game. One down within 15 minutes, Spurs fought back to bring the aggregate score to four – three in Benfica's favour. Spurs hit the woodwork three times and had dubious decisions given against them. Finally, they were out – but only until the next season!

Despite their involvement in Europe, Spurs went on to beat Burnley three goals to one at Wembley to qualify for Europe once again, this time in the European Cup Winners' Cup competition, not as prestigious as the European Cup and only three years old, but nevertheless growing fast in world standing. Riviera was now deeply involved in Spurs' success. We travelled to Glasgow, Bratislava, Belgrade and finally to Rotterdam for the final against Atletico Madrid. This final tested our organisational ability to the limit.

On the strength of all we had done over two years of involvement and in anticipation of what was to come, we moved into empty premises in Bishopsgate. This included a ground floor shop with offices above. And as soon as I had put a package together we were inundated with people anxious to book – by telephone, telex or personal call, every plane that we could charter was fully booked as soon

Tottenham Hotspur European Cup Winners' Cup team, 1963.

as it was put on sale. I spent long days searching for further capacity and in the meantime a queue would gather from early morning until we closed at night. Many waited patiently for news of available seats, a lot of them were youngsters, ten or eleven years old, clasping their £8 and ten shillings in their pockets. Bishopsgate resounded to cheers as groups slowly moved nearer to the front of the queue. With 33 aircraft booked and 2500 passengers, we had at last to call it a day. Rotterdam airport could accommodate no more and I had used up all the spare aircraft capacity available! We utilised 65 coaches at both London and Rotterdam to transport fans to and from the various airports. We lost no one in the transfers and there was a minimum of drunkenness and rowdyism. Spurs won five goals to one on that memorable day, 15th May 1963, and Riviera went on to become a major tour operator in the south east.

Michael and I left the ground early to ensure everything was in hand for the return journeys and missed the final goal. We were, though, euphoric if slightly battered because of the over exuberant passion of the game. We needn't have had any fears – lined up in a splendid row were the 65 coaches displaying our company name and logo prominently on the windscreens. We only lost one sup-porter who, overcome by it all, plus one or two drinks too many, chose a coach from a company in Limburg, where he landed having slept through the journey. He called next morning for assistance and this was duly provided. I had to smile proudly, as I recalled my impotent envy at the queues outside Martin Rookes and Skytours in the early days.

The success we had in organising the travel arrangements for Spurs' supporters encouraged us to set up a similar programme for England supporters in the run up to the 1966 World Cup, and this we also did successfully. It was at the final in Wembley Stadium that I first encountered the unbridled nationalism, indeed tribalism, that eventually moved me away from a game that had been a major part of my life. The atmosphere was not just intense, it was fervently fanatical and bludgeoning, to the extent that I could easily imagine myself at a Nazi rally. It was a similar feeling to that at the Spurs v. Sunderland game, when our small group had feared for our lives. Our travels with the Spurs' supporters, though, was always a genial affair, and there was a warm comradeship on every trip. Even at Benfica, when we lost, we spoke approvingly of the Portuguese players. You always wanted to win, but the game itself was the thing to be enjoyed to the full.

Much of Riviera's publicity work was undertaken by my good friend, John Gorman who, apart from his other talents, ran an excellent printing business. He often did the work jointly with Ken Sprague from the design and graphics company, Mountain & Molehill. One of their major serious commercial contracts was the publicity work they did for my company, Riviera Holidays, in the mid-sixties, when they produced a number of our brochures and created some very effective advertising and agents' campaigns. These included a bonus scheme for agents, a defining logo and a major scoop in persuading Bobby Moore, his wife Tina and young daughter, Roberta, to take one of our holidays.

We already had connections with Bobby through our work transporting England supporters to away matches abroad, in the run up to the World Cup of 1966. It was in 1965, when John negotiated a deal with Bobby, that in return for a holiday and a small remuneration, we could use photographs of him and comments by him in our brochure the following year. This was at a time before footballers of his stature could command millions for commercial deals as they do today. Riviera organised and paid for two holidays for him and his family, in 1965 and 1966.

The brochure production included photographs of hotels and resorts, and this is when Ron joined the team. The shoots were at all our resorts and the team included one or more models, and the inclusion of some of our guests. Ron was no Adonis − of medium height, with a ready smile, a droll humour, and a great listener, when he would sometimes cock an ear as though he had a hearing deficiency, but he clearly had charms for the opposite sex.

He was an endearing, softly spoken and beguiling man, and he also had a shrewd ability to judge the potential of people. We became great friends and he

Meeting Bobby Moore, 1965.

was a frequent visitor to our home. Since we remained totally unaware of how he exploited these qualities with the women, it was clear that he could also be very discreet. It all came out, when an irate husband finally cornered him.

I was awakened very early one morning to hear a voice say: 'Aubrey, have you ever known anyone who was murdered?' I was stunned into silence. I supposed that this question excluded my war experiences. It was John Gorman, and I replied somewhat perplexed, 'No'. 'Well you have now,' was his reply, 'Ron was killed last night'. I was stunned, and all I could say was, 'where, when and how'. 'Where would you think?' he queried intent on keeping me in suspense. 'In a lady's chamber?' I responded, flippantly. 'Exactly!' he confirmed. While Ron was a sad loss to us, I feel sure he would be missed just as much by his many lovers.

CHAPTER TWENTY
A new sales agent, with a silver touch

Riviera's growth was outstanding even within the exceptional travel world we now lived in. Our representatives in the Italian Adriatic for that first year were provided by Martelli but we did need a courier to travel with the Smith's party. My thoughts turned to a young man in my Communist Party branch who had once been on holiday to the Adriatic with Intertours and was therefore, among the select few who had travelled abroad, so could be considered almost an expert! Sidney Silver was at that time employed by a company offering discounted white goods and cars to trade unions. Despite our disagreements on several aspects of party policy, I respected his intellect and education. He'd spent many hours in our flat so I knew him well, and he lived in the block next to us. After considerable discussion and much persuasion, he eventually agreed to take the party. While he knew no Italian, he spoke French, was adaptable and, most importantly, he was the only person we knew we could trust.

On the day, we met on Victoria Station – and I can still recall it most vividly – the three of us, Joe, Sidney and myself stood around a small high table in the bar having a beer. Sidney showed his unease, and belatedly wondered how I'd persuaded him to take on the job, and me insisting, time and time again, that I had done all the work, signed the contracts. 'It will be easy for you', I said, 'nothing can go wrong'. Well, that was on Saturday morning, on the following Monday morning I was in the tiny room that was our 'reservation centre' when I took a phone call. It was Sidney: 'Nothing can go wrong!!', he rasped in the sinister tone that I learned later was the way he expressed his anger, 'nothing can go wrong –

when we got to Calais we found that the French farmers had gone on strike and we had to hang around for hours, and then, when we at last got to our hotel, we were told it was full!'

The amiable Signorini had double booked and double crossed us. Fortunately, our agent, Martelli, could provide rooms at a new and superior hotel directly on the beach in a quieter part of town. The hotel had opened two days previously, with only a small number of rooms taken up. The staff welcomed the group, so despite the initial hassle all ended up with a better deal.

I congratulated Sidney on finding a solution, and suggested he just relax and enjoy the remainder of the holiday. However, his travails were not over yet. On the return journey, the Italian railwaymen were on strike, causing yet another delay. We had many lessons to learn, and the most important was: don't tempt fate, or not too often. Despite the problems, the response from the group was favourable and Sidney could take most of the credit. He'd managed to exploit to the full his charm and sociability.

A major decision we later made was to make air travel the basis of our programme, and this decision was key. Next was to persuade Sidney to join us. This was not an easy thing to do. If we had encountered difficulties getting him to take the Smiths' group, it was like climbing a mighty mountain to get him to join us full-time.

Joe arranged lunch at his house in Loughton and throughout the meal and into the early hours of the next day we employed our vision and all our enthusiasm. The former, more than the latter, persuaded him to consider. Finally he asked for another few days before making his decision, but eventually, after another session with me while wandering the streets of Stamford Hill, we reached an agreement.

Sidney was a grammar school boy, who over the years as a single man had gathered a singular cultural knowledge. He was an excellent mimic, a singer of original cockney songs and had the fantastic ability to reach out to people. His critical knowledge of football, theatre and films served him in good stead but most importantly it also served our company. He became without doubt the most successful sales agent in the business and served as the front man for the company. He traveled the country making personal friendships which persisted long after Riviera. If he had a fault, it was his inability to make decisions. We soon learned that his indecision about joining us was very much an intrinsic part of his character; it was even true in his love life. There were several times when he was a step away from marriage, only to cry off at the last minute. Yet he valued the company of the ladies and his successes in this area were many. He also became a lover of good food, something he was unable to control, and which became an important contributory factor in his early death.

For the first time I now had someone with whom I could discuss things other than Joe, who was too involved in his own accountancy business. Joe's contribution to Riviera was not hands on. Sidney, on the other hand, once installed, became deeply involved. The knowledge he gained from visiting agents was invaluable and helped us formulate policy.

It was during a discussion on policy that we decided that we could not restrict ourselves to a small minority of local agents plus the personal contacts that I and others made. Consequently, we went into Joe's office to explain that if we were going to get anywhere we had to go national. The argument was heavy, but finally Joe agreed, but only that we take on no more than one hundred agents – this was ludicrous, and we ignored him.

Riviera grew rapidly yet the total number working for us was still minimal. In the very early stages, prior to my full time working, I shared a three legged table in Morrison's office with my sister, Sheila Steele, who was Morrison's part time secretary and Ray Swart a youngster of 16 years who was articled to Joe. Ray's ambition to become an accountant was diverted into Riviera, along with Sheila, who eventually became our reservations manager.

Almost immediately we were compelled to move offices to rooms above yet another Barclays Bank, almost next door to the Bishopsgate Institute on the corner of Spittle Street and Bishopsgate. We immediately began the recruitment of additional staff.

Hazel Hoffman, formerly in charge of reservations at Horizon, joined us and set up a comprehensive and manageable reservation system which was vital. Sheila James was poached from Bon Viveur and these were followed by a number of young people, none with travel experience, but soon enthusiastically involved. They were all important, particularly the switchboard operator through whom all calls were then channeled. Gloria Johnson and later Margaret O'Connor were the first introduction to Riviera when agents or their staff called. They were successful in setting the tone by this initial contact. So much so that they were soon on first name terms with most callers. The personal touch was a vital ingredient for any successful travel business – the 'family' effect.

The hundreds of different brochures received by agents were enormous, and most received no racking on the shelves or exposure in windows. The front covers were not dissimilar – either of people sun worshipping or of a spectacular view. One coach operator, Silvio's Italian Tours, in sheer desperation, put a photograph of a Gorilla on its front cover. Unfortunately the owner, Silvio Ballasio, was killed soon afterwards in a car crash, so we had no indication of the success or otherwise of his marketing ploy.

Several operators collapsed during the early years and their clients were left stranded unless other operators, having spare capacity, stepped in to salvage things as best they could. Failures could be attributed to all the factors enumerated above plus over ambition, wrong resorts, bad hotels and poor administration. The pitfalls were many. Generally the companies were not corrupt but the industry was crying out for a means to overcome this ongoing problem.

The method of keeping and winning agents used by the establishment was usually an annual dinner, sometimes with a dance and cabaret for their best or potential agents, and this would often involve an overnight in a posh hotel. During the course of the evening the MD would give his opinion on the health of the industry, congratulate his guests on their collective ingenuity in supporting his company and would see no reason why they would need to change.

In 1961 George Jackman, a well known character in the travel industry, left his position in Hotel Plan to join the family Mantagazza as MD at Cosmos, a new coach tour operation. George was blunt and very much to the point in his language and his down to earth attitude. For many years his annual get-together was one of the highlights in the travel agents' social calendar and the company grew, but eventually as it began to concentrate more on air travel and set up its own airline, George was sidelined into near oblivion. Sidney Silver was one of his successors.

Riviera could not compete with that kind of extravagant expenditure, nevertheless it was important that we kept contact with the coterie of agents who supported us. I decided that since it was impossible to bring them to London, a small group of us would visit them. We arranged gatherings of agents, both those supporting us, and those we aimed to win over, in each of the major cities in the country. We provided nothing lavish, just a buffet with drinks.

Sidney Silver was in his element on these occasions since he either knew them from personal visits or through numerous telephone calls. He remembered each and every one, but more than that, even the particular football or rugby club they supported and often intimate details of their families. My responsibility was to discuss the trade prospects and Riviera's programme for the coming year. Others who were important included the reservations manager and switchboard operator, because in those days the first voice agents would encounter would be the young lady (in those days they were all female) who over time provided useful information for agents and their staff. These gatherings became a very successful part of our marketing strategy.

Familiarisation trips to countries and resorts were usually offered by tour companies to proprietors and senior management; staff were not usually included. The idea was that if you won the hearts and minds of the hierarchy, they would see that your product sold. We looked at it differently — we involved our staff at the highest marketing level and learned from their contact with the selling staff of our agents that this was where the driving forces lay.

Our first educational, as we preferred to call such trips, was a large one. We took two coaches of travel people, one for seniors and one for counter staff, on a visit to Italy. Using an empty aircraft for our outward journey, we flew them to Nice airport from where they traveled along the Riviera to our hotel at Pietra Ligure. There they spent some time looking at hotels along the coast, being wined and dined by hoteliers with lots of time relaxing, following which they were driven across to the Adriatic coast, where they enjoyed similar hospitality with a final dinner in the ballroom of The Grand Hotel in Rimini hosted by the Adriatic Tourist Board. It was an excellent function with speeches, really distinguished food and wines. It was a tremendous success and firmly established Riviera as a substantial company.

However, ailing companies became an ever increasing problem for the industry and there were growing demands for increasing security. Of course the larger operators, well established and seemingly secure, were all for draconian measures, while at the same time they were afraid of government interference. It was the collapse of a heretofore unknown operator 'Fiesta Tours' that was the catalyst for controls to be instituted albeit on a voluntary basis.

To the trained and experienced eye, a glance at the expensive glossy brochure put out by Fiesta Tours for the 1964 summer holidays was incomprehensible. Hotels were recognisable but all flight timings appeared to be the best and most convenient. The giveaway, however, was the lack of airline information and flight timings in the brochure. No matter the strength and influence that accrues with wealth and standing, it was virtually impossible to put together this kind of programme. The venture had been the brainchild of a Dutchman, Jan Schildkamp, who it seemed, had put out a similar version in Holland. There were no flights, and members of the public who had entrusted their holiday plans to them were left stranded. The events were further complicated by Schildkamp and his associates' attempts to transfer the responsibility for the whole fiasco by selling the operation, (and falsely representing the true financial position of the company) to a Mr. Henry Whitfield, who at 79 years of age, and with sufficient wherewithal was desirous of obtaining a serious foothold in the industry.

On January 19th 1970 at the Old Bailey, Ian McClennan was jailed for 12 months, and accomplices, Patrick Collis and Nicholas Langley Pope, who admitted conspiracy, were each given suspended sentences of 12 months. Schildkamp, it was said, had disappeared with £20,000 of Fiesta's money. This episode forced the industry to look more closely at the problem and with an additional operator failure later that year, the Association of British Travel Agents initiated the first move towards protection. It was Charles 'Tubby' Garner, then the chairman of ABTA, who organised the rescues for the stranded Fiesta customers in 1964 and following his untimely death his successor Dennis Hopkinson, out of fear of government legislation, set in motion a satisfactory consumer protection scheme for its clients

ABTA was having other difficulties too. The rule of membership which forbade members trading with non-members was being overwhelmingly flouted. The new operators who were unable to obtain ABTA membership were providing a product most called for by the general public. Additionally, an alternative organisation, The Travel Trade Association, had been formed to provide what the public could recognise as providing equal surety to that provided by ABTA. Basically, they provided a visible organisation and, of utmost importance, a logo to put in the agents' windows and on brochures.

It was under Garner's successor as chairman, Desmond 'Hoppy' Hopkinson, that the association decided something had to be done. The requirement was to retain ABTA as the sole organisation representing the trade and maintaining its exclusivity. They decided on the obvious: making membership easier by dispensing with antiquated criteria, and in this way embracing TTA members and others, while at the same time applying alternative standards, more applicable to the changed circumstances. Travel agents could become members providing they had been trading for at least three years. This ensured the registration of all established travel agencies and tour operators. A fund to safeguard stranded passengers was set up and all members were required to contribute through increased membership fees, and levies when necessary, but not exceeding 50% of those fees. 'Stabiliser', as the scheme became known, was adopted at the 1965 convention and, once applied in January 1966, saw the membership of ABTA more than double by 1967. The TTA became extinct almost immediately. Nevertheless Stabiliser was not entirely welcomed by a large number of ABTA members. There was no doubt that Stabiliser was born out of fear of government legislation, however for all its faults it gave dominance to ABTA and set in motion a satisfactory consumer protection scheme for its clients.

The air charter business was all about numbers. It was about getting bums on seats. If it was costed correctly and the aircraft filled, you made a lot of money. Fly them empty and you lost much more. Certain flights were easily sold: school holiday periods, Wakes weeks (a phenomenon in Northern England where all the factories in a town would close for two weeks) – all were in the period of late July and early August. So if you had a series of flights that included too many outside those periods, it was always a struggle to make the series pay. This is where having a multiplicity of sales outlets was important, but it was not easy to achieve. Our core of producing agents was based mainly on those we'd assisted in starting up. Our direct sales came from recommendation; our advertising budget was negligible and initially was sometimes insufficient to enable the chartering of full aircraft and we had to share with other operators. I quickly became aware of the pitfalls in doing this. Your partner or even partners might not be able to fulfill their obligations which then put all the flights in danger. So choice of partner was important.

I was asked if I would attend a proposed flight consortium meeting at Luton Airport. It was a tripartite meeting and all things moved smoothly until we stopped to have a bite before formalising the deal. The others were two well-seasoned operators and they began to regale me with stories of their past associations: because sales over the August Bank Holiday and surrounding dates were always buoyant they would overbook these departures. It was customary to do this to cover cancellations that always occurred and which would normally be dependant on the size of the aircraft – around four percent. However these two gentlemen would continue to book just as long as people wanted to go. This meant that come the day, they found they had sometimes double the numbers, which meant that many passengers had to wait as long as 48 hours till they could be found empty seats. I was aghast at this attitude and left in near panic.

Relatively easy to start up, the considerable potential of this new and adventurous business attracted people from all walks of life, and I was one. Another was Vladimir Raitz of Horizon, often acclaimed as the father of the air-package holiday. He built a travel empire from an original idea of air charter holidays to a tented holiday camp in Calvi on Corsica, operated by a group of Russian émigré friends. It was probably because Raitz had been granted a group charter, which had never happened before. Licences were granted for 'affinity groups'. In that instance passengers were limited to students and teachers.

Raitz soon overcame the group obstacle and was granted licences to fly members of the public to destinations where BEA did not operate. The venture started in late May 1950 but the series lost the £3000 start-up money Raitz had invested, and that was a considerable amount in those days. The following year the venture proved successful and Horizon Holidays moved into Majorca and became one of the most prestigious and profitable of all the air holiday companies.

The discarding of older aircraft by the national airlines rapidly increased the number for charter, which in turn fed the growth of tour operators and travel agents. The exponential growth of holidaymakers, not only from Britain but from Germany and Scandinavia too created a scarcity of hotel accommodation at the popular resorts and precipitated an era of heartbreak hotel stories.

CHAPTER TWENTY ONE
It's plain, it's got to be Spain

In the early stages of our operation we had concentrated on Italy. However it became obvious that the major growth area would be Spain. Our past made us reluctant to operate in a fascist country particularly that of Franco's Spain. Memories of those traumatic years remained. My views were changed through a chance meeting with Maurice Haskins, a veteran, spending most of his life in Spain, who had an involvement with a small British tour operator, Vista Tours. He made a courtesy call on me during which we discussed the question of dealing with a fascist country, thereby assisting its economy.

He argued with emphasis and example that tourism was one way and a serious one in which Franco, or any other dictator, could be marginalised. He felt increased contact with other countries, improving the people's standard of living, while at the same time raising their aspirations and giving them a vision of something better, was a worthwhile goal. He suggested that I make a visit to the Catalonia area, around the Costa Brava, to check it out myself, and suggested names of people who could guide me.

Lily joined me on the flight to Perpignan in France, close to the Spanish border. The only other airport that could be used by charter flights into that area of Spain was Barcelona, but since this was a route used by BEA, no charter flights were licensed. Hiring a car and driving along the coastal route we were amazed and immediately attracted by the coastline and the tiny atmospheric fishing villages.

I recalled having read a book by Norman Lewis in which he described an episode, not on this particular part of the coast, but similar, further south of Valencia. Oranges for marmalade making were brought to ships close to the shore in barrels on tumbrel style open wagons pulled by horses. His description of the struggle between the driver, his horses and the rolling waves was dramatic. In the process of traveling through the sea the barrels containing the oranges filled with sea water which, as they traveled to their destination — perhaps Scotland — gave them an exclusivity in taste, regarded as a valuable culinary asset.

Estartit and Rosas were places already in the Horizon programme and had an air of exclusivity not suitable to our type of operation. Tossa del Mar appeared to have been taken over by Germans and was therefore discounted. Lloret de Mar was almost exclusively British and seemed an obvious choice if we were to operate anywhere. We traveled on as far as Barcelona, where Maurice had arranged a meeting for me with an agent whom he recommended.

Heretofore our hearts and minds were Italian, but the journey we had just completed, the rugged beauty of the coastline, and the friendliness of the people we met, captured our imagination. By the time we reached Barcelona we were almost convinced that we should start operating as soon as possible. Pepe Salva had left a message at our hotel that he would call at 10pm for dinner. We were convinced this was a mistake, but sure enough he arrived at that time and the evening was about to commence. We had never experienced such late night eating or the crowds that appeared like magic, filling the streets with colour and noise, so late in the evening. It seemed that the whole of the town had converged on Las Ramblas with the sole purpose of strolling around and holding animated converstions. Soon the couples and groups peeled off into one of the many restaurants and tapas bars that lined the surrounding streets.

For us there was a real gastronomic experience ahead. When we arrived at the restaurant it was empty apart from two or three secluded tables at which youngsters were sitting and appeared more interested in each other than in the food before them. Not so for me. Part of the evening in Lisbon, prior to the Benfica game, had been in a restaurant at which I was introduced to eating lobster and I now welcomed every opportunity to relish the fresh seafood. We were soon introduced to Paella Valenciana and squid — another not to be forgotten experience. I find I can best remember places and people through my palate and intensive culinary delights. Even today this is the case, and that meal in Barcelona was truly memorable as was another that we had at the restaurant Las Caracolas which, in sharp contrast to the superior and dignified ambience of the previous evening, was very low key, with sawdust on the floors, ageing and knowledgeable waiters and a boisterous, noisy clientele.

The following days we used inspecting and choosing hotels. Lloret was obviously a boom resort with new hotels being built seemingly overnight, yet obtaining sufficient hotel beds to take our aircraft passengers we still found extremely difficult. Pepe suggested we look at nearby Calella, a small, quiet resort. We first looked in on a Sunday afternoon and in the village square people were dancing the Sarzana, the national dance of Catalonia. A large circle had formed which fluctuated in size as people joined in or fell out. It appeared as though a few people decided to have a dance while encouraging anyone else wishing to join in.

Calella was much the same style as Lloret but much more tranquil and relaxing. It was uncommercialised and devoid of tourists. The hotels were smaller and family run which was similar to many of the hotels we were already using in Italy. We were more fortunate here and had no difficulty in obtaining the beds we needed. Calella eventually became one of our popular featured resorts. True enough Spain became the major destination for the British holidaymaker and the Costa Brava became the main port of call for first bookers.

In the same year I visited Majorca for the first time. Arriving at 3 am I was overcome by the heat of the terminal which was nothing more that a tin hut. As the passengers tumbled out into the near dawn and moved to their coaches, I managed to get a taxi to take me to Arenal the nearest recognised resort. I was put down in what appeared to be a desert with just about seven or eight hotels. I was depressed at the enormity of the task I had set myself. I walked from the far end of El Arenal, through Ca'n Pastilla and San Jordi into Palma much of which was like trudging across a desert.

I'd arranged to meet an agent, Don Ricardo of Airtours, at the Bahia Palace in Palma that morning and I could only hope he had something to offer. If I needed anything to convince me that the people of Spain's attitudes and customs were changing, meeting Don Ricardo exemplified what Maurice Haskins had told me. He was a dapper little man, dressed in a white suit and shoes to match, with a gold topped walking stick and an air of importance and arrogance. I was given the unmistakable impression that he really was doing me a favour and that he had in fact made a mistake in meeting me at all, something that should have been left to an underling. Later I did meet his assistant, Frank Juame, a cheerful local man who had worked for some time in the PX at an American forces base and consequently spoke English with a harsh US accent. He very clearly resented the high and mighty attitude of his boss. Nevertheless he still addressed him as Don Ricardo, as did other staff and, as I saw later, did all the locals.

I always found it difficult to reach out to the Don and I soon realised his appointment made by the Swiss headquarters of his company some time ago was a relic of a fast disappearing custom. An aristocrat provided the prestige 'name plate' while the workers did the work. Despite all that, once we got under way,

Ricardo set up a number of hotel visits, which I carried out, accompanied mostly by Frank, and which enabled me to put together an attractive programme.

There was an exponential amount of hotel building taking place in Spain, particularly on the Costa Brava and in Majorca, where new resorts were being initiated. A major factor in the equation was the Spanish custom of primogeniture, whereby the eldest son was entitled to the major assets of any inheritance; the other relatives were left with diminishing rewards. Spain at that time was an agricultural country and consequently the land was split between the sons accordingly. The youngest and probably the most poor, would inherit land nearest the sea. Until the advent of tourism there was little he could do with it, but then came tourism and this land became very valuable.

Soon the impoverished landowner also recognised that there was an alternative to selling − consortia were set up to build hotels. Alternatively the landowner could borrow the money on a variety of securities. There were deals with tour operators, guarantees of occupancy and advance payments. Hotel building became a major industry and a new breed of hotel proprietor and manager was born, sometimes with calamitous results.

Lack of controls in building, or finance delays caused late openings which in turn reflected on the tour company's programmes not only in the UK but also in Germany and Scandinavia. Insufficient knowledge of management and shortage of kitchen staff also created difficulties. Hence the holiday horror stories that periodically gained prominence in the national press. Nevertheless there were numerous success stories. 'From bus boy to owner of one of the world's largest hotel chains', was one. All this created ripples in the hitherto rigid class structure. Everywhere hotels were being erected in a frenzy of building activity. And they were becoming larger and larger, with more and more beds to satisfy the exponential demands of the holidaymakers. Building Riviera necessitated an ever extending programme and soon it was Benidorm on the Costa Blanca and Fuengirola, Torremolinos and Marbella on the Andalucian coast.

On one of my trips to Palma, I met by chance Robert Waley who had a small tour operation. He confided in me with great excitement that he had found the next great Majorcan resort − Calamillor. He had produced a simple black and white leaflet outlining what he claimed was then the only hotel on the beach − the Pension Neptuno. This he claimed would lift him into at least the second division of operators. Unfortunately the very long distance from the airport was along secondary roads and without sufficient numbers the cost would have been prohibitive, as indeed proved to be the case, and he failed. Along came Langton already in possession of the three nearby hotels at Cala Bona and, hey presto, success.

Members of Riviera staff at Southend Airport, I am third from right and Sidney Silver second on my right, 1964.

The number of passengers we were carrying grew ever more. It necessitated Riviera securing more and more hotel beds and this required greater involvement than ever envisaged. In Cattolica, still our bedrock, I agreed to guarantee the leasing of the Hotel Britannia for Fabio and Anna Baffoni, newlyweds wishing to enter the hotel business. Fabio's parents ran the small pension Enrici and it was at their request that I agreed to sponsor them. Fabio, from being a lorry driver, became an excellent hotelier and sophisticated Anna from Florence a driving force. This was the way it was. And from all this grew many other personal friendships.

During the Spurs and England supporters' campaign we had had occasion to use Channel Airways based at Southend Airport. It seemed a logical progression that as an East-of-London operator we should make Southend our base for operations. At the same time we flew from Gatwick and a limited series from Manchester. Using one airline for the major part of our flying, it was thought, would ensure added negotiating strength.

Channel Airways was the brainchild of Squadron Leader J. R. (Jack) Jones who had started the airline while still in the RAF in 1946. He bought three Puss aircraft, cannibalising two to make one air-worthy, and flew short joy trips along the Kent coast from Herne Bay in the name of East Anglian Flying Services. It was from this that he progressed to Dakotas and Vikings, flying from newly-opened Southend Airport. He set up and operated several short haul flights to Ipswich and other smaller airports in East Anglia. Among his most profitable routes were the Channel Islands and Rotterdam in Holland. Hence the name change to Channel Airways.

It was when Channel acquired a number of Viscount aircraft from British European Airways that I became really interested in the idea of putting most of our eggs in that basket. By 1965 we were flying 43,000 passengers on Channel's 'Golden' Viscounts and became his major, if not the only, operator of substance to holiday destinations.

Jack Jones was an irascible and obstinate person to deal with. I suppose he saw me as just as difficult and our negotiations were almost always close to physical. What he gave with one hand he tried to take back with both, and our association was always contentious. In 1965 he set up his own tour operation, Mediterranean Holidays, persuaded our general manager to join him, leafleted our passengers, and used any empty seats and also our empty legs to carry his few passengers. That ended our association. The following year we used the aircraft of Britannia Airways.

We were forever seeking new countries, resorts, hotels and occasionally modes of transport. Within a short time we had extended our range to Yugoslavia, Ibiza, Rome, Sorrento, the Venetian Riviera, Morocco and Greece. We were offering select club resorts in Majorca, Morocco, Greece and Yugoslavia. Like all travel companies, we were successful in some areas and not in others – we were subject to fickle swings of fashion, even in those early days.

Sidney Silver became the contact in some countries – Yugoslavia, the Venetian Riviera and Greece were his domains. It was as a result of his contacts in Athens that he was introduced to Costas Ephtymiados who had an idea to revolutionise cruising in the Mediterranean. As we understood it, he was a lawyer who had married well, and had aspirations to become a shipping magnate. At that particular time smaller tankers were being replaced by craft of much greater tonnage. It was his idea to scoop out the innards of such outmoded ships, leaving the engine, which was in the rear of the ship. This allowed the maximum space to build rooms in the fashion of a hotel, with a large expanse of deck. It appeared to be a great and innovative idea. All rooms the same; the only difference would be the number of decks. This would overcome the problem of different classes and room styles. Maybe he was the inspiration for fellow Greek, Stelios Ioanna, and his 'one class' Easycruises. He had already built one ship, the Helleana, which he was using as a ferry on a route from Ancona to Patras.

So we tried an experiment, but since the price of holidays to Greece was high, we decided to fly into Milan Airport. From there, guests would travel by coach to Ancona, transfer to the Helleana for an overnight cruise along the Adriatic and return with full board accommodation for 15 days at a cost of 69 guineas. The operation was successful and we decided to continue working closely with Ephtymiados on expanding the cruise holiday idea.

By this time we had extended the idea of receptions for proprietors and managers of travel agencies around the country, with a morning session for staff at which we provided either a breakfast or lunch. At these sessions I would go through the brochure explaining our programme, talking about resorts and hotels, fresh ideas, our booking procedures, where to book the elderly and so on. This would normally take the whole morning.

At one such gathering in London, at which nearly 300 were present, Ephtymiados burst into the hall. He was a handsome man well over 6ft tall and as well-built as Adonis. And he had an eye, if not two, for the ladies. He was Anthony Quinn personified, and his gestures and ready embraces took everyone by storm. His next ship, the Sophia, he told us, was to have its maiden voyage the following month, on the route to Crete, when it would begin regular operations carrying passengers and essentials that up till then, the island had not been receiving. He would be on the first ship to perform a Godfather ceremony for all the children on the island who had been named Costas during the past year. If he had said that he had fathered them all, we would have believed it. 'You are invited to join me, all of you', he said in a final flourish of generosity. 'Leave your name and you will receive an invitation.' We were all flabbergasted.

It was a coup for us, although we would be committed to provide the transportation. The cruise turned out to be memorable for all who went on it. The stories that came back were far fetched, I thought, but they proved to be true. The wine flowed and the food was plentiful. Costas played the host in true Greek fashion, excelling himself in every way. Unfortunately his high living and lack of control in his shipyard, then a fire on his flagship ferry the Helleana, all combined to scupper the idea at the time. However, it was resurrected decades later with the building of purpose-built cruise liners carrying thousands of passengers.

CHAPTER TWENTY TWO
Our company at the crossroads

Riviera grew rapidly in status, carrying ever more passengers and employing more staff, and this now required departmentalisation: sales and reservations, accounts, overseas hotels and transfers, and representatives. The quality of reps. was vital, yet our selection process was still primitive. It was largely based on intuition or urgent need, sometimes both. On reflection, this also applied to the people on reservations who were mostly very young, often in their first jobs. They all went through fire and brimstone, which was part of working in this new travel industry and with very few exceptions they enjoyed being there. They were making history and, just like Langton and Raitz, they too were pioneers. There were also opportunities to travel — whenever there were empty seats, they could have a weekend away. Long lasting friendships were made throughout Britain and in Europe.

Unfortunately, as often happens, with our success also came dissension. Joe Morrison and I, friends for so many years, became fractious with each other. I was devoting myself to Riviera totally, whereas Joe was either unable or unwilling to do so. In the early part of 1965 he told me that we were incompatible and he wanted out. Either I buy him out or he would sell his share of the business, he said. He named a price which even if it had only been ten percent of his figure, I could never have raised the money. So he then told me he had a buyer for the whole business. Without my knowledge he had been approached by Raitz of Horizon on behalf of the Thomson Organisation, who were in the process of buying Skytours and Britannia, and the price being offered was exactly twice the amount he was asking for his share.

This came as a bombshell and caused me considerable grief, as it did my family, close friends and colleagues, but there was no apparent alternative. By this time the relationship between Joe and me had hit rock bottom. We only exchanged the odd cursory word relating to the business. While I have no doubt that my obsession with Riviera, to which I had devoted so much over those past years, had made me a demanding person. I expected others to feel and do as I did, and while this expectation may have been an inappropriate approach for some of my colleagues, I thought such an attitude absolutely essential from a partner.

The four of us — Raitz brought along Gordon Brunton, a joint managing director at Thomsons — met for lunch and discussed the deal. I remained very much a bystander. I had no idea beforehand who the prospective purchaser was and it was only at this moment that I ws informed. Thomson's, owned by Lord Thomson, was a media conglomerate which had recently taken over *The Times, Sunday Times* and *The Scotsman* as well as other smaller newspaper groups. But one of his most important and remunerative undertakings was the new Scottish Television franchise. Lord Thomson in his own blunt words declared that the television franchise was a licence to print money, and so it was.

On 1st April 1965 it was announced in the press that Thomson's had entered the travel business with a vengeance. Why he wanted Riviera, I only understood once the deal came into force and we were actually operating as one organisation. It was obvious that the purchase of Skytours and Britannia were the really important acquisitions. But that's the way capitalism works — the urge to create a monopoly and buy out all competition.

In the end we had to sell, there was no other way out. I spent that evening with my family, a few colleagues and friends with a cheque in my hands for a sum of money I had never ever imagined I would see, let alone possess. Yet we were all in tears. This was not the way it was supposed to be. I hadn't gone into this business for the money, I did it because I enjoyed it and I was proud of what we'd been able to build up. Of course money was essential, but having a load of it was not my prime goal in life. I felt my baby, my creation, had been ripped away from me. I had also lost a long time friend, without whom the whole project would never have been born. Joe came out of it extremely well, and Sidney Silver, to whom we had each given shares, when we made him a director, was also amply rewarded.

Part of the deal was that I would remain with the new company and It was shortly after the sale, that I was offered the job of MD at Thomson Travel. I'd only had just over five years of full time work in the industry and here I was being offered the job of head of the largest tour operating company, certainly in Britain, if not in Europe. I accepted. I decided to hand in my bill that I had worked so assiduously to obtain, but I held on to my qualified cab driver's badge to keep my feet on the ground.

At first the only difference to my routine, was the necessity of attending board meetings, where I met other senior people in the organisation. It was soon apparent to me, though, that the boardroom was a virtual war zone. I was never at any time made aware of the chaotic conditions that then existed in the company, or of the task that I was about to undertake. I never knew that at the board meeting which finally decided to purchase Skytours and Riviera, negative and damning reports from Thomson's auditors had strongly criticised the financial management of the company. As Vladimir Raitz writes in his and Roger Bray's book, *Flight to the Sun*: 'According to this report, financial control was non-existent, the company was running at a loss. There was no coherent management structure whatsoever, and every single decision was taken by Captain Ted himself, who appeared to be a complete maverick. The only positive aspect was Britannia Airways, which was professionally run by Jed Williams and later by John Sauvage, an old aviation hand. But the airline at that time was a relatively small part of the whole.'

In his autobiography, *After I Was Sixty*, Lord Roy Thomson wrote of that decisive board meeting: 'The project was presented to us by Gordon Brunton in the boardroom of Elm House. He had called the accountants to examine the balance sheets and the projections, and to give their views of the proposals. We had found an opening in the travel business fairly early in its developing story; this can be judged by the fact that Skytours had not yet shown a profit. Nor were there any assets other than three or four Britannia aircraft; only goodwill and shrewd faith. I don't think I have ever heard a less favourable report than that which the accountants gave that day. In our three hours' discussion, a great deal was said about what could go wrong with Gordon's scheme. I did not say anything until all had been aired, and then I said I wanted to go ahead with Gordon's scheme. He had the idea that ordinary people would go for aircraft travel. We went into the travel business.'

I was installed in South Audley Street which was not an ideal place for me since I felt very isolated. There, I found that I had inherited a PA, one Lionel Steinberg, and a number of other staff for whom there appeared to be no work at all. To introduce the organisation to the travel agents, a lunch was held at the Royal Lancaster Hotel at which the guests of honour were Lord Thomson and the English football captain, Bobby Moore. I was the main speaker. With considerable discomfort I read my speech, something I normally hate doing. When

Me and the Guv'nor – Lord Thomson in 1967.

I finished I put it down and spoke off the cuff to the agents about the problems we had and how I thought the trade could develop and about the problems we faced: the competition for hotel beds, the importance of new aircraft, and the question at the forefront of all agents' minds – commission. My remarks were well received, and the agents gave me a standing ovation. It was then, if not before, that I realised why Riviera had been purchased. It was to have me as the safeguard if relations with Langton did not work out

It took many months of struggling to cope with all these problems while at the same time trying to expand the business. There was the ongoing and additional need for extra beds, but also the need to retain those whose allegiance was either to Langton or myself. Coping with unfinished hotels, attending regular board meetings, as well as involvement with Thomson's solicitors, Allen & Overy, over hotel contracts, which they always wished to examine at great length and trying to ignore the ambitions of individual Thomson loyalists fighting on two fronts was very stressful. Reconciling marketing needs under Harry Henry and the burgeoning activists under Brunton was a nightmare. Brunton needed a speedy success to justify his purchases. The tasks were really daunting and I did-n't feel comfortable with them, because neither they nor the solutions demanded were of my making. I was invited to lunch by Brunton one day, to be introduced to 'my new chairman', Hilary Scott. He was a man with a famous surname, but with a most unprepossessing manner. My cockney friends would have described him as 'not knowing his arse from his elbow'; he was a relic of the colonial empire.

It was not long after this meeting, that I was forced to resign, and there fol-lowed at least four, if not more changes in managing directors within the follow-ing year. Most resigned after a short space of time, so I was clearly not the only one who couldn't work in that atmosphere. Thomson's did finally find an MD who succeeded where so many of us had failed. He was Brian Llewellyn, and he contacted me almost as soon as he was appointed and we met regularly for lunch at Quo Vadis in Dean Street, the building where Karl Marx had once lived. We talked about Thomson's and the travel industry in general. I really don't know why I did this, but probably because I felt flattered that this bright young man thought that he could learn something from me.

One of the few perks that came my way while I was MD at Thomson's, was a visit to the Soviet Union. Offers of testing long haul destinations or specialised educational tours at that time were still aimed at management, but I had always been so heavily involved in my day-to-day work that I had never accepted any until 1968, I was offered a place on the inaugural Aeroflot flight from Heathrow to Leningrad. An added incentive was that Lily was able to come too.

My only experiences of travel to eastern European had been day trips to Zabrze, in Poland and two visits to Czechoslovakia, none of which, despite my membership of the Communist Party, had made me wish to return for any length of time, so it was with some trepidation, but also anticipation that I accepted.

The flight itself was of no great significance but the food, drink and service were exceptional, far better than Aeroflot's later reputation would suggest. There were 22 of us on board and included in the party were a number of journalists and travel agents. Of particular interest to me was meeting and spending some time with two of them. They were Phil Piratin, the former Communist MP for Stepney, and Frank Gullitt, a grizzled, but jovial reporter for the *Daily Worker*. Apart from his political activities, Phil was also chairman of Progressive Tours, the Communist Party-supported travel company specialising in tours to Eastern Europe, and it was in that capacity that he was on board. He was a garrulous individual and able to talk about and discuss at great length most subjects.

By the time we landed at Leningrad airport we had been well fed with caviar, sturgeon, smoked salmon and, of course, as much vodka as we could take. On landing, we were ushered into a fairly bare hall except for a long table on which there was yet more food and drink. We were greeted individually by a man who I supposed was the equivalent of the general manager, only this man was a real general with all his medals, including the Order of Lenin, emblazoned on his uniform. He was a veteran of the war and had been a leader of the defence of Leningrad, and he proved to be a delightful raconteur with a fund of stories with which he regaled us through an interpreter, in between glasses of vodka that he downed in one gulp and a toss of the head, as the Russians are wont to do. This vodka drinking continued through all the speeches. This, it turned out is very much a Russian tradition and, to avoid becoming legless before it's all over, you need a gut of steel. This time, there were exactly 44 toasts, since there was an employee of the airport to match each one of us, and each had to propose a toast to something or other. I just about remained upright, and was glad I didn't have to drive my cab into Leningrad.

We were driven into the city, past all the destruction and devastation left by the war, still very visible all around us. I had seen bomb damage in London and in western Europe but not having visited Dresden or Coventry, two of the worst hit cities, it was difficult to make a comparison between those and what I was passing through here — an almost total devastation. In the city centre, though, the damage was less obvious, as already much rebuilding had been done in an attempt to return Leningrad to its previous glory.

It was early spring and the glowing pastel shades of the buildings and their sharp outlines reflected the clarity of the air. The numerous ornately-decorated cathedrals and churches, surmounted by golden domes and the wide expanse of the Neva River provided a breathtaking panorama. The guide travelling with us had all the statistics at her fingertips and gave us all the information we needed, in a charming and friendly manner. Without exception, we were all stunned and overawed by the grandeur of the city. When we stopped on one of the canal bridges, our guide described in graphic detail moments from the terrible seige of Leningrad. We were wrenched back to the reality and significance of the battle that had raged in and around the city during the most significant period of the Second World War.

The facts are awesome: two million residents held out for 900 days from September 8th 1941 until January 27th 1944, living virtually without food and no outside supplies. The citizens ate anything and everything that moved. Almost a million died. And it was obvious that our guide was talking from first-hand experience. Whereas the general, in his own jocular fashion, had talked of his exploits and those of his heroic comrades, her commentary was more sober. The heroic sacrifices of Leningrad's people reminded me of the campaign we on the left had unsuccessfully waged for the opening of a second front to alleviate the fierce fighting and intense suffering endured by the Soviet Union as a consequence of Nazi invasion. It was Churchill who said that the Russians, particularly in the battles of Leningrad and Stalingrad, 'had torn the guts out of the Nazi Army'. Several of us shed more than a tear on hearing about these events first hand.

I am not a great admirer of churches and cathedrals, other than to wonder at the immense amount of labour and craftsmanship that went into building them, but it was easy to be overwhelmed by the grace and beauty of the many that abounded in this elegant city – the 'Venice of the North'. The canals and the river did indeed remind me very much of the real Venice.

Of all the wonders of the city, though, the Hermitage art collection was the most splendid. I have to admit that I had not had the time to visit many museums in my busy life, and I suppose, in that respect, I could be considered a philistine, but the Hermitage changed all that. The works of Rembrandt, Titian, Leonardo da Vinci. Rubens, Picasso, Renoir, Gauguin and even Gainsborough hung alongside the works of so many other great artists, filling and spilling out of each and every room. Then there were the rooms dedicated to the splendours of Tsarist Russia and the Winter Palace. We also paid a visit to the battleship Aurora, which had played such an important part in signalling the beginning of the October Revolution.

We were also taken through the narrow streets, in which so many of Russia's eminent authors had lived and written their world-renowned works, and we also visited the house in which Tchaikovsky had died.

An amusing observation for me was to see a film director we met, who was of an older generation, drinking lemon tea through a piece of cube sugar between his teeth, as it reminded me of my paternal grandfather who had always done the same. The actress accompanying him behaved in a more genteel manner; she flavoured her tea with a spoonful of dark jam. Both, though, smoked incessantly, also a very Russian custom.

It was unfortunate that our stay in Leningrad was limited to only two full days, as was our stay in Moscow. We entered the latter by coach, but first made a stop by a monumental memorial of a Red Army soldier in full battledress, some six miles from the centre. This was the spot where the Nazi army had been held in its tracks, before being forced to retreat in another critical moment of the war.

Our hotel in Moscow was the National. It was rather drab, being one of the older hotels, and still retained the traditional Babushka caretaker seated on each floor. We spent little time in the hotel, though, in order to use our limited time to see as much as we could of the city. Lily and I wandered off on our own on several occasions. I was particularly intrigued by the bakeries and the styles of bread and cakes that were sold. It brought back memories of my family's bakery, the smells and tastes of my childhood. In many ways they were very like my grandfather's early bakery with what were then called 'continental' products. Black, rye and plaited loaves abounded, alongside a large variety of rolls and different varieties of brioche yeast cakes. There were very few cream cakes of the sort so prevalent in Western Europe. The other shops were full of both goods and customers, but the method of payment was antiquated and not dissimilar to that used in Foyle's bookshop in London. You queued to choose your purchase and were given a numbered ticket to queue again in order to pay and have the ticket stamped, then queued once again to collect your purchase! This irked Phil Piratin, who, ever the businessman, immediately worked out what he would introduce to make things more efficient. We were happy enough to go through the procedure, though, to have our cakes which we munched lovingly.

Lily and I differed in our first impressions of the people we saw. I was very taken by the manner in which people greeted each other with small posies of spring flowers, like freesias. Lily was more observant and noticed the overwhelming aura of sadness that seemed to hang over the people with whom we were, unfortunately, unable to converse, although there were no restrictions on our movements or on who we could or could not meet. Sadly, we both had no Russian, so were unable to converse with people on our own.

The highlight of our stay in Moscow was our visit to the ballet. We were given seats as a group to see *The Fountains of Bakshiara* in the huge and magnificent Palace of Congress, where the Bolshoi's first ballet company was performing. The Bolshoi theatre itself was being renovated at the time. The hall in the palace seated 6000 people and had sufficient escalators to empty the auditorium to the refreshment room above in ten minutes flat. The building had been designed by Michail Posokin and opened in 1961 in time for the 22nd Congress of the Soviet Communist Party of that year. The seats were opulent, but ticket prices were affordable. Looking around the audience, the few who were dressed rather exclusively were obviously Americans, some of whom I spoke to later. They were amazed at the performance and performers, the building and the audience of ordinary Muscovites. Also enjoying the performance on that evening was a British parliamentary delegation led by Cyril Black, a doyen of the Tory hierarchy and with whom Phil renewed his acquaintance.

Frank Gullett preferred to visit a Greek Orthodox Church. It was a Friday and a service was in progress. Being a true atheist, he was prepared to ignore the religious connotations in order to hear the wonderfully evocative Gregorian chant. His absence left me with an empty seat next to me.

The ballet told the story of the Tartars' invasion of Russia. The scenery was opulent and the exquisite dancing beyond belief. Towards the end of the first act I suddenly found a man seated in the empty seat. I was a bothered a little when I noticed he had a small parcel wrapped in newspaper on his lap. I thought he would open it in the interval and bring forth some garlic-filled sausage or something similar, which would distract me from the performance. But I was soon once again absorbed in the ballet on stage. Towards the end, one of the leading ballerinas was clearly about to perish, and performed a movingly tragic dance sequence before she metaphorically died. As she made her bows before an enthusiastic audience the man by my side stood up, went forward to the stage, stood there looking directly at her for just a few seconds then unwrapped his parcel from which he drew a small bouquet of flowers and flung them at her feet. Another last glance at the stage and he was away. We never saw him again. I could remember nothing about him except his shabby coat and his determination. Ever since we've always wondered who he was. Maybe a separated father, a banished lover or infatuated balletomane, we shall never know.

We did the things all tourists do: visited Lenin's tomb, went on the metro, and were impressed by how spotlessly clean and how regular the trains were, then on to the Kremlin and the GUM shopping store. We did a small amount of shopping, but most of our time was spent just walking about and observing.

Those of us on the group in the travel industry had a long session with Intourist managers where we discussed the possibilities of improving tourism to the Soviet Union. As the MD of Thomson's I was called upon to give an opinion. Obviously there was a tremendous potential but the Cold War cast its long shadow over any East-West undertakings. Intourist promised that there would be newer and better hotels. They would get rid of the persistent touts trying to buy dollars, and they promised to impress their own Intourist managers to be more flexible in dealing with their counterparts in Britain, and overcome the rigid manner in which they operated. They would also improve the quality of the food. We ate some meals in the hotel and they were very much of a standard similar to those served in the lower price category in Britain. Unlike most of the others in the group, I was more acquainted with the type of food served because of my East European background so was not disconcerted by it. To the others, the combination of foreign flavours, bad cooking and carelessly served meals was very off-putting.

Despite the obvious problems, I wanted to help. I understood better than most the difficulties that still remained following the enormous damage and suffering left by the war, but I also understood the fortress mentality that had arisen largely as a consequence of the aggressive attitudes of the USA and its

European allies to the Soviet Union. I promised that we would make every effort to promote tourism and to get things underway I immediately suggested to Sidney Silver that he should undertake a more long-term assessment of the possibilities. He duly went off with a planned itinerary agreed with Intourist. He was away for almost five weeks, but kept in touch with reports until the last two weeks when we heard absolutely nothing from him. We contacted Moscow, but they too had lost track of him. He finally arrived home bright, chirpy and laden with little gifts and told us he'd visited a state farm in Georgia organised by Intourist. Knowing what Georgian hospitality was like, I could imagine how he'd been wined, entertained and dined and been reluctant to leave! I have already written of his ability to get on with people but he also had a facility with languages and he very soon improved on the little Russian he remembered from his parents who had originated in Odessa on the Black Sea. He'd got on so well in Georgia that he was asked to stay on. His guide was called away and, without knowing what arrangements had been made with the farm leaders, he just stayed put until one of our many faxes caught up with him. He had a tremendous time and he told us about it with great relish. I never read his report to the overseas department, but despite his growing disenchantment with communism and the Party, he went overboard about the tourist possibilities. He influenced Thomson's, albeit belatedly, to start a limited Russian programme.

CHAPTER TWENTY THREE
The new Africa — a time of optimism

'...It is particularly important that we should now understand the connection between freedom, development, and discipline, because our national policy of creating socialist villages throughout the rural areas depends upon it. For we have known for a very long time that development had to go on in the rural areas, and that this required co-operative activities by the people...

When we tried to promote rural development in the past, we sometimes spent huge sums of money on establishing a settlement, and supplying it with modern equipment, and social services, as well as often providing it with a management hierarchy... All too often, we persuaded people to go into new settlements by promising them that they could quickly grow rich there, or that Government would give them services and equipment which they could not hope to receive either in the towns or in their traditional farming places. In very few cases was any ideology involved; we thought and talked in terms of greatly increased output, and of things being provided for the settlers.

What we were doing, in fact, was thinking of development in terms of things, and not of people... As a result, there have been very many cases where heavy capital investment has resulted in no increase in output where the investment has been wasted. And in most of the officially sponsored or supported schemes, the majority of people who went to settle lost their enthusiasm, and either left the scheme altogether, or failed to carry out the orders of the outsiders who were put in charge — and who were not themselves involved in the success or failure of the project.

It is important, therefore, to realize that the policy of Ujamaa Vijijini is not intended to be merely a revival of the old settlement schemes under another name. The Ujamaa village is a new conception, based on the post Arusha Declaration understanding that what we need to develop is people, not things, and that people can only develop themselves...

Ujamaa villages are intended to be socialist organizations created by the people, and governed by those who live and work in them. They cannot be created from outside, or governed from outside. No one can be forced into an Ujamaa village, and no official – at any level – can go and tell the members of an Ujamaa village what to do together, and what they should continue to do as individual farmers...'

Julius Nyerere, first President of Tanzania

After I left Thomson's, and before becoming involved in the retailing operation, I was approached by several organisations, some purely commercial and others dedicated to the eradication of poverty, working with tourism. When the Tanzanian Tourist Office invited me to visit their country to give advice on the possibilities of developing tourism, I accepted with enthusiasm. I suggested to Lily that she come along and that we also visit Ethiopia and Kenya on our return journey.

The emergence of the new African states following the reluctant transfer of power by their former colonial masters engendered an early enthusiasm in me. I had been horrified, that despite strong independence movements and a clear demand by the mass of the people to be free, these colonial masters continued to assert their power on the African continent. This led to the deaths of many progressive leaders such as Lumumba in the Congo, Cabral in Guine Bissau and Machel in Mozambique, s well as the vile treatment of others like Kenyatta in Kenya. It was in this climate that the behaviour of Nyerere in newly liberated Tanzania excited me, for here it seemed there was a serious and potentially successful attempt to create a socialist country against all the odds.

Dr. Julius Nyerere was born in 1923 in Northern Tanganyika and went to school only until he was 12 years old. When he was 20 he attended the renowned Makerere College in Uganda where he obtained a diploma in education. In 1949 he went up to Edinburgh University, in Scotland, from where he graduated with a Masters in economics and history.

When he returned to Tanganyika to teach, he was acutely aware of his people's increasing thirst for independence. He also saw clearly that without a forceful and effective leadership their hopes would remain just that. He immediately joined the Tanganyika National Union, the main nationalist party, and soon after became its leader. It was under his leadership that the country eventually obtained independence, and without bloodshed, leading to a smooth hand-over of power. This was an incredible achievement, given the turbulence and instability pertaining in many other African countries.

He embraced all peoples who had made their home in Tanganyika, as newly born citizens of the new Tanzania, creating a truly multi-ethnic and multi-faith state. He was an avowed socialist, who was courageous and determined to end racism and internecine strife and raise the living standards of all his people. He said: 'We are determined to maintain our mastery over our own destiny – to defend our national freedom. We are determined to change the condition of our lives. It is to meet these two needs that we must have both change and stability. These two must be inter-related for neither is possible without the other.'

Nyerere established a number of principles which needed to be put in place, if tourism were to fit in comfortably with the overall future plans for Tanzania. Among them, his view of safari trips was clearly outlined and his views were amazingly perceptive at a time when ecological issues were little recognised: 'The survival of our wildlife is a matter of grave concern to all of us in Africa. These wild creatures amid the wild places they inhabit are not only important as a source of wonder and inspiration but are an integral part of our natural resources and of our future livelihood and well-being.' In his influential Arusha Declaration made in 1967, he called for a 'made in Tanzania' variant of socialism, including full rural development, genuine self-reliance and the abolition of corruption. His concept was bold and comprehensive. Unfortunately, subversion by western capitalist countries combined with widespread internal corruption undermined his vision. It was obvious to me that within the context of his plans, seeing tourism as an integral and non-damaging part of the country's economy would require greater controls than most western travel entrepreneurs would desire.

The major investor in the country at the time appeared to be a hotel company, Hallmark Hotels, which either owned or controlled most hotels throughout Africa. I was advised to seek out John Skinner, their representative, who had lived some time in the country and who would be a useful source of advice. I met him some days after my arrival and his advice was indeed useful. Sunday, the day of our arrival, after the tedium of a long flight, was quiet and relaxing in Dar es Saalam. One could appreciate Nyerere's concern about creating a unity of peoples. I had not expected to see such a large number of Asians here; dressed in their finery, they could be seen parading along the promenade outside our hotel. It was easy to deduce that these were mostly relatively wealthy traders and could well become, as happened in other African states, a future source for resentment and discontent.

Soon after our arrival in Dar es Salaam, I realised that the Israelis were also involved in the tourist business. Our hotel had been built by the business arm of the Israeli trade union, Histradrut. I later learned that they were also involved in major road building projects in the country.

We were assigned two young male employees from the Ministry of Tourism who had a wealth of knowledge and were not averse to providing an opinion on most issues. Our first visit was to Silver Sands, a recently developed resort on the coast. This had been on the route Livingstone had taken on his expedition and close to where the slaves, when captured by Arab traders, had been transported to the Americas.

Conveniently, it was a national holiday on the day we travelled, but even so there was little traffic on the road. During the journey I saw what I thought was a witch doctor surrounded by a crowd of people. Intrigued I urged our driver to stop. Reluctantly, he reversed until we came level with the group. It was indeed a witch doctor who appeared to be exorcising a woman seemingly close to exhaustion. On noticing us, he came forward holding a long encrusted wooden ladle which we realised was filled with a most uninviting liquid. Lily was alarmed: 'I can't drink that', she said, but he came on with dogged determination. One of the young men told us not to worry he would deal with it, which he did with a few words and salutations plus a sip of the concoction. Once back in the car, both our guides declared that having been away from their villages for some time they were disconcerted at being involved with witch doctors. Lily of course berated me for asking them to stop.

Silver Sands was what could be termed a purpose built resort. There was no village nearby that was part of the complex. It consisted of a number of standard resort buildings on either side of the main bars and restaurant, set directly on the broad, sandy beach. It was obviously very popular and there were a number of Europeans and Americans mixed with local people, most of whom were young. It could have been anywhere – the Bahamas, Majorca or the Costa Brava.

I was introduced to the proprietor who, not surprisingly perhaps, was named Silver (hence the name of the resort). He and his two brothers were Israelis and had been involved in the original road building programme. His brothers had returned but he had stayed on to develop the resort. It was from one of our guides that we learned of the vast coral reef that lay offshore, and also that Silver was an avid collector, both legally and otherwise, of corals. He later showed us his collection, collated and stored in specially constructed drawers.

We did not have the time to investigate for ourselves the beauties beneath the Indian Ocean but noted the tourist opportunities it offered.

Next day we flew to Zanzibar, and for me this was to be the highlight of the tour. Incorrectly I had always associated Lon Chaney's film, *West of Zanzibar* with that island but of course its very name contradicted the idea. Nevertheless I was very excited about being there. This was at the time when, despite an agreement in 1964 creating a union between Tanganyika and the Island to form the Republic of Tanzania, there was still considerable hostility between the Sheik who controlled the island, which was overwhelmingly Muslim, and Nyerere with his secular ideas.

It was difficult for the Tanzanians to put into place here the reforms so essential to the principles outlined in the Arusha Declaration. Yet there were constant and on-going discussions without threats at all levels, attempting to find solutions. And the reasons for some of the problems were clearly discernable. Driving through the narrow streets it was clearly a population made up of a mixture of Arabs and Africans, but the cultures of these two peoples were very different, as we learned during our stay. But for the moment I was transported by the heady aroma of spices that penetrated every nook and cranny. The streets and shops were more Arabic than African and as we drove further into Stone City the differences between the two cultures became ever more apparent.

Our hotel was the Dhow Palace situated in the heart of Stone City, which enabled us to set out immediately by foot through the narrow streets. It was evening and we followed behind a crowd of people entering a vast square, at one end of which there was a huge elevated stand on which there was a large number of musicians carrying a variety of instruments, of which we could recognise very few. Ours were the only white faces in the square.

I have to admit that I am the archetypal seeker of the true travelling experience; I wasn't interested in a facade set up purely for tourists, I wanted the real thing. Otherwise what reason would I have to listen to a music that was unfamiliar and, for us, difficult to identify with and in a language not a word of which we understood. The first singer went on for almost an hour singing, what appeared to us, to be one song, with verses adapted to the requests of people in the audience who made surreptitious donations to the players.

The next day was spent exploring this fabulous island, with its pristine sandy beaches merging into the azure waters of the Indian Ocean, and softly waving palm trees lining the horizon. I had my camera, together with three lenses (this was before the zoom lens had become a standard accessory). Some of the local boys were more than willing to climb the palms barefoot for me to photograph. I am probably the most incompetent photographer and my skills had not moved beyond the box camera, so naturally when the lad reached the top I found I had the wrong lens on the camera. I felt ridiculous shouting to him to stay up there until I could change my lens, in a language he would not understand. Needless to say, my photos were hardly colour supplement material.

Returning to Dar es Salaam, we stayed overnight, before setting forth on a safari early the next morning. Our first destination was Lake Manyara National Park, one of the smaller of the many parks in the country. Elephants dominated the wildlife and we saw literally thousands of antelopes, some Thomson, but mostly impala. Accommodation was of a reasonable standard and the transport was comfortable. We had time for only one night's stay, before moving on to Ngorongoro Park within which there is a large volcanic crater. Ngorongoro was once an active volcano, which collapsed inward leaving a 'calder' which is the largest intact and non-flooded crater in the world. Here there was an even greater diversity of animals, among which, I was told by our guide, were the elusive white rhinos. They may have been elusive to others but I managed to come away with a whole number of slides of rhinos in different positions. For me the flocks of flamingos were among the most magnificent sights. In flight, the enormous flocks transformed the sky into a pink cloud. The Maasai tribe also live in this park, and even in those early tourist days would only allow themselves to be photographed if paid − but then, why not?

After five days away, we set out back to base, but not before stopping at historic Arusha, a city living in the glory of Nyerere's declaration and its consequent recognition worldwide as an important crucible of Tanzania's aspirations. We then moved on to Moshi to view Mount Kilimanjaro, only to find it, as so often, shrouded in cloud.

Our meeting with John Skinner was held in his office almost adjacent to our hotel, which indicated that his company was probably managing the place. We exchanged thoughts and ideas, and I put forward some of my own ideas to test his reaction. He suggested we go to Mafia Island, which he thought could be a prospective tourist haven. There was also another reason though. His wife and her sister, who also lived in Tanzania, operated a business exporting animals as pets to Europe and the UK. Once or twice a year they travelled and called on their clients. After several visits they had become friendly with a woman pet shop owner in a Northern industrial town of Lancashire. Over a cuppa they suggested that she should travel back with them and see where the animals came from. After much pressure she did, leaving her husband and teenage son to run the business. After spending some time visiting Tanzania and seeing much of what we ourselves had seen, she was persuaded to visit Mafia Island. The resident owner and manager of the Mafia Island Club was called Kos and was born in

Liverpool of Greek Cypriot parents. He had been a superb athlete, and was reputed to have been of Olympic standard in swimming and sailing. During the war he had been part of a small group who raided small Greek islands occupied by the Germans. The pet shop owner, like in a Hollywood movie, predictably fell in love with him and refused to go home. In fact she was still there and we were about to pay her a visit.

We were fascinated and intrigued by this romantic love story and during the flight in the small aircraft, in which the pilot almost sat on our laps, we wondered what this Greek Adonis would be like. The flight was calm and smooth and the vast expanse of the Indian Ocean below us was exquisitely therapeutic. Landing on a narrow strip of grass appeared to be no trouble for our experienced pilot. Kos was going to be there to meet us but we could see no bronzed athletic type waiting. There were a couple of cars to which other passenger made for, but all we could see was a dilapidated old jeep at the back of which stood a short, rotund bald-headed and bare-chested man in tattered shorts. As he came over to us, we realised that this was our man – so much for the Adonis image.

The drive back to his place was at break-neck speed over what was a very rutted, but solid road. We were bumped and shaken about like marbles in a tin, to be eventually tipped out in front of a shack on the beach-front, and realised that this was the club. Our room was equipped like the worst possible guest house imaginable and although there was a bath, there was only a dribble of water, and what there was of it contained a menagerie of insect life. Before we could take full stock of our surroundings, Kos knocked on the door and asked if we would like to go fishing from the club boat. This was not a trip for pleasure though; food was required for the evening's meal and we had to catch it!

There were five members of the crew from Sabena Airlines, who were waiting between flights, and all of us walked to a ramshackle, but sturdy wooden pier to take the boat. It was most exhilarating gliding across the ocean, with each of us taking a turn in the fishing seat. We returned with a beautiful rainbow-coloured, monster sea bass. Our initial feelings of a disaster were dissipated by the meal and the beer. And despite all our fears of being eaten alive by insects or visited in bed by other sinister creepies and crawlies, we slept well.

We awoke to a symphony of birdsong and a decent breakfast, after which we strolled across the grass lawn for a dip in the warm Indian Ocean. We eventually met the wayward lady from Lancashire, and Lily was told the whole story of the love of her life. One phrase she used stayed with me: 'Look at me now, look where I live and then think of me stuck in a pokey little shop on a miserable rainy day in the heart of Wigan!' There was little to argue against that.

I looked further along the beach at a large house situated almost at the water's edge, that was, apparently, for sale on a 99-year lease for the modest sum of £2000. I was tempted for a few moments, but reality soon grabbed me by the collar. We flew back to Dar-es-Salaam and the next day we were due to leave for Addis Ababa.

On each morning during our stay in Dar es Salaam we saw children in large numbers walking to school. All the girls had smart and crisp, white blouses and green skirts, the boys wore shirts and green trousers. Most had made long journeys from villages, undoubtedly without electricity, certainly without washing machines or any other modcons, but all were turned out as if they lived just around the corner in a London suburb, but were overjoyed to attend school, unlike so many of their British counterparts. As someone who has always valued education this was a lasting memory. How vital education would be in these countries, if they were ever to attain real independence and raise their standards of living.

My report on the trip? There were of course clear incentives for tourism: some of the most beautiful beaches in East Africa, fabulous surrounding islands for diving on the coral reefs, perfect weather, and national parks teeming with probably the largest variety of animal and bird life on the continent. To open it up to general tourism would undoubtedly create lots of problems. One was the logistical one of getting there; infrastructure − roads and transport in particular would require massive investment and where was that to come from? How would all this fit in with Nyerere's concept of integrated tourism? He called for and planned a 'made in Tanzania' socialism, with rural development, self-reliance and ending corruption. The sagacity of his leadership had meant that Tanzania was spared the extremes of misery and violence suffered by her neighbours. Nyerere's economic programme, considered rigid and naive by many in the West, was nevertheless effective.

The need for heavy outside investment would only facilitate outside interference in major policy matters. These were difficult choices. For example, when gold was discovered below Lake Victoria by tribesmen in 1976, it was followed by an influx of artisan miners and their suppliers. Very soon between 30,000-40,000 Tanzanians were employed as gold miners in the area, and small businesses and local entrepreneurs proliferated. During the period from 1990-94, the Bulyanhulu artisanal mines produced the bulk of Tanzania's official gold exports which averaged US $30 million per year.

Kahama Mining Corporation (KMCL) itself stated that the artisanal miners in Bulyanhulu, paid taxes and levies which were used for community development purposes, such as the construction of two classrooms for the Kakola Primary School. In general, the small-scale mining activities over the 1975-96 period 'raised incomes, increased population and stimulated services, such as transportation and shops. Before the later closure of these small scale mines, the average income in the study area was the highest in the Shinyanga region.' Following interference by the IMF, pressures were put on the government to let in the multinationals, and the whole operation fell into the hands of a big Canadian-owned company. KMCL goes on to say that 'after cessation of artisanal mining in Bulyanhulu, in August 1996, the income of the majority of people declined significantly, the populations of Kakola and other villages in the Ward of Bugarama decreased, and services either worsened or disappeared.'

How far can lone socialist ventures, like Tanzania's succeed within a capitalist dominated world? Nevertheless at that time we were both uplifted by our Tanzania experience. It was a tranquil, but exhilarating place to be, and several times we said half-jokingly to each other: 'let's stay'.

How different was Ethiopia and Kenya. The former was drearily and terribly cold. We spent one miserable night in Addis and on the next day headed for Asmara, the capital city of Eritrea, in the hope that it would be better, and it was, in certain respects. The food was Italian orientated, but we were appalled by the disparity of wealth between the local people and the colonialists. Walking back to our hotel, we passed numbers of rag bundles in the streets — these were human beings, destitute and without a roof over their heads. One we saw was a very young girl suckling a baby, both completely naked, covered only by a thin sheet, on an almost freezing night. After Tanzania we found all this difficult to stomach.

After leaving Ethiopia, we arrived in Kenya and spent one night in Nairobi. Kenyatta Avenue reminded me of the line in that old socialist musical hall song: '...and the walls were made of marble...' Each bank, and there many from most of the Western countries, were extravagantly and lavishly built. We were warned about crime, which even then was rife, and told not to go along River Avenue, and urged to take maximum care during our stay.

I made the point earlier with regard to the political consequences of mass tourism on the peoples of a country. In Spain it had enhanced the lives of the indigenous people and in Italy too, but those countries largely kept control of the developments. During the time of Apartheid in South Africa tourism was of no benefit to the native population at all. In Kenya, too, we felt it was out of their control.

What has happened to the travel industry since was inevitable; it's symbolic of capitalism. It has moved away from the single entrepreneur and is now, with very few exceptions, run by technocrats and managers of big companies who have allegiance only to their own pockets, and there is little innovation anymore.

Everything has been tried before, sometimes successfully, sometimes not. We now have vertical integration: direct sales, low cost flights etc. and of course changing technology and improved communications have played an important role. The ecological impact of mass tourism is only now, and belatedly, being cautiously raised. I had already broached this question at an ABTA conference as early as 1972, but, predictably, it received little attention. In this area, the industry still appears to be almost completely blind.

CHAPTER TWENTY FOUR
Birth of the Anjou Club

K hrushchev's cataclysmic speech to the Congress of the Communist Party of the Soviet Union in 1956 sent shock-waves around the world. In the wake of his revelations of Stalin's horrendous crimes and what he and his cohorts had inflicted on the Soviet Union and indeed the whole world Communist movement, the Communist Party of Great Britain found itself in an ongoing and serious crisis. It became very much a party of two warring factions — a hardline pro-Soviet wing and a Euro-Communist or reformist wing.

It became increasingly clear that it would be impossible to reconcile the two, and a split occurred — most of the leadership and the majority of the membership discarded the party's traditional title, CPGB, and renamed it Democratic Left. The hardline section split away to form the Communist Party of Britain (CPB) and managed to take the Morning Star (formerly Daily Worker) with them. Although the paper was nominally owned by its readers, in the form of a co-operative, it had always taken its editorial line from the CPGB and was considered to be the Party's paper. This meant that Democratic Left had no paper of its own, so after much deliberation, the idea of founding a new weekly paper emerged.

John Gorman, a close friend and managing director of a print company, and I were both approached by Michael Triesman to promote this new weekly newspaper, appropriately titled, 7 Days. It was to be launched by a group of left intellectuals, including Anthony Barnett, Fred Halliday, Phil Kelly, John Hoyland, John Matthews and David Triesman, then firebrand son of Michael, with the involve-

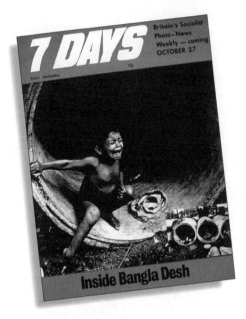

Selected front covers from the short-lived weekly *Seven Days.*

ment of Stuart Hood, Gareth Steadman-Jones, John McGrath, Claude and Alexander Cockburn and Jenny Moss.

It was to be a paper in the style of the defunct *Picture Post,* published by Hultons. This magazine in its heyday had been extremely popular and been an effective contributor to political thought and discussion during the 1930s. *7 Days* would be in black and white and also have a large photographic input as counterpoint to the written word to give it the feel of an open, airy paper, not one of dense, impenetrable text. The paper ran for a number of issues but, sadly, after a relatively short life, failed for a variety of reasons.

Having agreed to provide a substantial financial contribution, we decided to celebrate the venture. I mentioned to John that I had three bottles of what was reckoned to be one of the finest wines ever produced – Romaine Conti. I had wanted to discover what it was like but had never had a suitable opportunity; this was as an appropriate time as ever. We spent the whole afternoon going through the recognised procedures for drinking such special nectar, and it proved worth while. The wine turned out to be an exquisite tipple and its taste lingers still, even if the paper which prompted its opening unfortunately doesn't.

John Gorman had been first introduced to me in a cafe opposite Dalston Junction railway station by Lionel Bart when I first started cabbing and on the very occasion I used the Dalston rank in Arcola Street. Thereafter, I would occa-

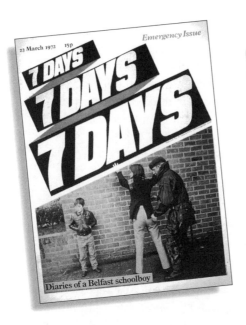

sionally be entrusted with delivering the finished sample products of window display material produced by John's small silkscreen workshop in Rokesby Street. Over the years we became great friends and allies in many a political and commercial venture.

John and Lionel had met in the RAF during their National Service. Lionel was an artist with thespian ambitions. John was an experienced silk screen printer with a wide knowledge of the many forms of print he had accumulated as an apprentice and in arduous evening classes. Both came from modest, East End backgrounds and were of similar leftish political persuasions. It was inevitable that their collective knowledge and abilities would lead to a commercial relationship, started on their release from National Service, in two basement rooms in Elderfield Road.

John in his autobiography, *Knocking Down Ginger,* explained how, having been evicted from their first premises because of the smell emanating from the inks they used in the printing process, they found a new 'factory': 'our first search among the columns of the *Hackney Gazette* led us to a studio at Dalston Junction, offered at a rent of two pounds a week. It was a dream. Situated in a small yard, the studio was built on top of a workshop occupied by a firm of surgical instrument makers, and looked like a set for the artist's garret in *La Bohème.'*

Times were difficult for them from the start, but by hard endeavour during the early period, they were now settled into a 'proper workshop' with reasonable equipment, instead of the make-shift contraptions they had been using up till then, some produced by John's dad, an experienced carpenter, using wood rescued from skips and rubbish tips. But Lionel, even in those early days, spent as much time as possible in the world of theatre, and anyone who saw his performance as one of the ugly sisters — certainly the ugliest I have ever seen — in Unity Theatre's renowned and highly acclaimed production of *Cinderella* in the forties, would have no doubt that this was where he belonged.

Lionel also wrote some of the lyrics for that production, a skill he had honed in his political cabaret work which had been directed and produced by Alfie Bass. At Unity he had been involved in only four productions, before he joined Joan Littlewood's Theatre Workshop company in Stratford East, where his first venture was to write the lyrics for the musical, *Fings ain't wot they used to be,* which eventually became a West End hit.

Bernard Miles, the actor and theatre entrepreneur, then asked him to write the lyrics for his opening production *Lock up your Daughters* at the newly opened Mermaid Theatre. Lionel also wrote the successful song, *Living Doll,* for Cliff Richards and other popular songs for Tommy Steele and Anthony Newley, but his greatest success was the musical *Oliver,* which is still being performed throughout the world, and there is a film version.

Lionel's lack of discipline, though, and his extravagant life style was exemplified by his having to sell the rights to *Oliver* for a paltry sum, prior to its opening. He thus never truly benefited from its huge success. All this theatrical involvement gradually distanced him from the work of the printing firm, G&B Arts. From working only three days and no nights each week, he eventually broke with the company completely.

From our early commercial dealings, the friendship between John and me became deeper and we each derived enormous pleasure watching the other's success in differing ventures. G&B Arts became recognised as one of the leading companies in its field and won many design and production awards, particularly for posters designed and printed for the Royal Shakespeare Theatre Company.

On a visit to Washington, years later, I went to Fogel's Shakespeare Theatre and was delighted to see several of John's posters prominently displayed in the foyer. John was a bon viveur. He enjoyed good food and fine wines with the occasional malt whisky to finish off the evening; he also loved travelling abroad and playing or watching cricket. As a member of Marylebone Cricket Club, he had access to the finest games at Lords and was an ardent follower of England's cricketers whenever he could, both at home and abroad.

He remained a loyal socialist till his dying day, despite his success in the capitalist market and his 'bourgeois' life style. In my opinion, it was his dedication to the National Health Service, established by a Labour government that, sadly, shortened his life. He was sent home from hospital, after suffering a serious heart attack, to await a date for an angiogram, which he knew to be urgent. I suggested that he should have it done privately — he could easily have afforded it — but it was his belief that having been treated so well while in hospital, the NHS knew exactly what it was doing. I seriously doubted, though, whether that knowledge alone could make up for the many other shortcomings in our treasured service that had been seriously underfunded and neglected by successive Tory governments.

At the moment of his untimely death, he was in the process of completing a book on the history of trade union posters in collaboration with Rodney Mace (the book was eventually published by Rodney). Despite his ill health, he decided to visit Caroline Benn, wife of Tony Benn, to photograph items she had in her collection, in connection with the book. It was this dedication that certainly contributed to a further massive heart attack shortly afterwards.

All his life, John had been deeply involved in the history of the British Labour Movement and in particular the visual representation of that history. His book, *Banner Bright,* on trade union banners, became a seminal work on this theme. And, as so often happens, it developed from a chance find during the time when John, in collaboration with the artist and poster designer Ken Sprague, was undertaking publicity work for the trade unions. Visiting one of the branch offices, John and Ken found in the basement a number of old disused banners. They were held in heavy wooden boxes and in surprisingly fine condition. They realised that there were probably hundreds more mouldering away in trade union branch offices and attics and that they would be lost to posterity unless someone did something about them, and quickly. John set out to find as many as he could and to photograph them for the movement and for posterity before they disappeared.

Describing to me his find and his intentions, I suggested he visit the premises of the Jewish Bakers' Union in Vallette Street, opposite the Hackney Empire. The last time I had paid a visit, they had no more than a dozen members, all somewhat traumatised because of the murder of their long serving and elderly secretary, Maurice Fine, who had been struck down during a robbery attempt. I recalled that they had a magnificent banner inscribed on one side in English and on the other in Yiddish. My father, during one of his disputes with my grandfather had left to work as a foreman at Rinkoff's bakery in Thrawle Street, and in order to get the job he had to join the union. To indicate which bakeries were unionised, each loaf had a small paper label indicating that it had come from a

The Golden 'Aub' award, designed by Ken Sprague, given to Riviera's long-standing hoteliers.

unionised bakery. My father, needless to say, did not stay long in the union.

John's book, *Banner Bright*, was greeted with approbation and was officially launched at an exhibition at the Whitechapel Gallery where many of the banners were displayed. It was opened by George Woodcock, the then General Secretary of the TUC.

John wrote two further books on Labour movement history themes: *To Build Jerusalem* and *Images of Labour*. His collaboration with the artist, Ken Sprague came about as a consequence of the break up of Ken's small advertising and promotional agency, Mountain & Molehill, dedicated to Labour movement work. It was so named in ironic reference to its two owners: Ken, who was short and stocky, and his partner, Ray Bernard, who was lanky and over six feet tall. Both had been stalwarts of the Communist *Daily Worker*. Ken as designer and cartoonist, and Ray as circulation manager.

Mountain & Molehill's greatest success had been to persuade the Iron and Steel Workers' Union to invite the Russian astronaut Yuri Gagarin, the first man in space, to Britain. The story is fully described in Ken Sprague's biography, *Ken Sprague — People's Artist*, by John Green. Not long after the company's launch it was already struggling to survive, and Ray decided to emigrate to Israel, leaving Ken to pick up the pieces. John Gorman recognised his plight and answered his plea to undertake joint ventures with him. Both saw this as a way of serving the Labour movement and, with John's commercial instincts, and his wide number of contacts, the company began to progress.

Mountain & Molehill's final contribution to Riviera was made in 1965, prior to the Thomson takeover, when I asked whether some kind of award could be devised, to be presented to our long-serving overseas hoteliers. Ken had the idea of a small statuette of the sun with surrounding rays which, when finally produced, he fondly called, 'the Golden Aub', in a play on my name. These were presented by me to the hoteliers of those hotels that qualified. At celebratory dinners, I made a cordial speech and gave due recognition to the award-winners. Unfortunately, after that our advertising was taken over by the Thomson organisation. Riviera lost its personal touch and M&M went out of business not long afterwards.

CHAPTER TWENTY FIVE
Old Friends and the Left in Crisis

A few years ago, my old comrade, Solly Kaye was in a mixed ward in a central London hospital for treatment of a kidney problem. It was visiting time and many members of his family were around him when a nurse called out in a rather stentorian voice: 'Solly Kaye is wanted on the telephone.' His daughter Joanna took the call and on her way back to his bedside she was accosted by a woman patient who, surrounded by visitors, asked her: 'Is that *the* Solly Kaye?' There were probably many thousands of people who in similar circumstances would have asked the same question, for during the immediate post-war years and until the break-up of the British Communist Party, Solly was among the best known members of his party as well as one of the best loved and renowned councilors in London's Tower Hamlets.

Solly became the leader of a small band of dedicated communist councilors, elected on to the moribund council in Stepney during the immediate post-war years. But which Solly Kaye did she refer to as she spoke to the people gathered around her? Solly Kaye the great orator, the man who took the collections at mass gatherings, using a fund of stories and jokes to extract significant amounts of money for the cause? Or the one who regularly, at Friday lunch times, stood on a soapbox at Tower Hill, expounding the communist cause, while exchanging banter with his audience of largely City gents, or exchanging genial repartee with Lord Donald Soper on an adjoining soapbox? Or was it the Solly Kaye, who throughout the years was an organiser and agitator, famous for a hundred or more campaigns on behalf of squatters or tenants harassed by landlords in

London's East End? Or was it Solly Kaye the teacher who spent so much time showing his pupils the joys of working in wood, the wonderful feel of the material, as well as the art of creating interesting sculptures from discarded pieces? Or Solly the book critic and polemicist? Or possibly Solly Kaye the artist whose work adorns the homes of his family and many friends. It might also have been, although I doubt it, that she recognised Solly Kaye t-he poet, one of the first to have his work displayed on the Tube, in the Poetry on the Underground initiative? Or Solly the lyricist who put appropriate words to 'Glory Glory Halleluiah' for Spurs' supporters to sing in those 'Glory Glory' days of the sixties.

Solly was one of those rare individuals who was talented in so many fields, as well as being a wonderful and warm human being, He was also a cartoonist who never bought a greetings card designed by someone else in his life. How he managed, despite an enormous commitment and involvement in politics, to be a family man and true friend to so many, is a puzzle, but he did.

He started out from very humble beginnings, as I did, and we had much in common, holding avid conversations on a wide range of subjects, continuing to do so even in the direst times, as when the Soviet Union imploded or when the Party was about to split. Solly, and so many like him, found it difficult to comprehend how such a wonderful ideal of a socialist society could turn into such a calamitous nightmare. Those like myself, who for various reasons had left the Party some time before, also tried to understand the events taking place at that time, and there were many theories about why and how it happened, but I feel sure none gave the full story.

The Anjou Luncheon Club

Although I had left the CPGB several years before the collapse of the Communist world, I was never one to abandon left-wing politics altogether. I wasn't one of those who drifted to the right, or became an armchair, champagne socialist. Left wing politics had been so vital a force during so much of my formative years that I was determined to find a niche where I could continue playing some part, however minor, in the struggle for justice and true socialism.

It was in this atmosphere, and wanting to open the discussion more widely, that I invited three other long-time friends to a lunch in October 1989 at the Anjou Café in Palmers Green. So it was that Joe Morrison, John Gorman, Sidney Silver and I initiated the Anjou Luncheon Club. A small group of like-minded individuals who would come together at regular intervals in a convivial atmosphere to discuss politics and listen to outside speakers address us on a variety of appropriate topics.

I think I felt instinctively that having a party allegiance could lead to a stifling of discussion, so we tended to invite people without such allegiances. To begin with, there was never any intention on my part to make it a regular event, but the friends I chose for the discussions were close, strong and determined in their opinions and after the first get-together, we decided to do it again the following month. Somehow the news of it spread like bushfire. John Gorman, in particular, brought in some of his own friends and I found others who were keen to join us. So, like Topsy it grew, and the lunches became a permanent fixture. They were always stimulating and lively occasions, with ideas and arguments flowing thick and fast.

Our opinions diverged on a range of issues, but our desire to know more, to bring together the knowledge and experience that we had accumulated through different sources over the years, made us anxious to continue to meet regularly each month. Others of a similar mind heard of our lunches and wanted to join us, until the numbers were too many to continue at the café, and, besides it wasn't private enough. So, it was decided that the Anjou Luncheon Club would move its deliberations to the Gay Hussar.

As a family we had been eating at the Gay Hussar in Greek Street from the day that Victor Sawa opened his Hungarian restaurant on the site. Over the years, it had become a well-known dining place for lefty politicians and others associated with them. I had often used the room on the second floor for small business and family gatherings because of the large round table there that could seat up to twelve people. To those in the know, it is called the Tom Driberg room, after the late, popular, left wing, and at times outrageous, Labour MP.

Our first meeting at the new venue was on Thursday 6th of February 1991 and we have met there monthly ever since. The information about this first meeting was publicised in our newsletter, *The Polemicist*. This was a period of intense discussion and debate, after the collapse of Communism and with the uncertainty on the Left and in the Labour Movement as to the way forward. Our speakers list reflected the diversity of subject matter and viewpoints.

Among our earliest guests was Anthony Barnett, co-ordinator of Charter 88, who opened on the objectives and achievements of his organisation and its structure. He questioned whether it was still possible for mass movements to influence political change. Will Hutton, Jo Durden-Smith, a British journalist living in Moscow, spoke at later meetings. Patricia Hewitt, then deputy director of the labour think tank the Institute for Public Policy Research, and now a leading minister in the New Labour Government was also a keynote speaker. Another stimulating and thought-provoking speaker was Hilary Wainwright, editor of the left-wing magazine, *Red Pepper*. I had been involved in launching the magazine in 1991 and have been a keen supporter ever since. I welcomed the emergence of an innovative and pluralist magazine of the left, and the Anjou

The Gay Hussar restaurant in London's Soho, popular venue for left-wing politicians and for the monthly meetings of the Anjou Club.

Club was always happy to welcome Hilary as a guest. Other speakers followed: Colin Ward, the well known anarchist and prolific author, Ed Balls, then the leader writer on economics for the *Financial Times* who, despite, becoming an advisor to the Chancellor, Gordon Brown, and now an MP, still joins us every year as does Larry Elliott, Economics Editor of the *Guardian* newspaper. Looking back over the years, our growing list of speakers reads like a Who's Who of the left in Britain.

Members also made their own contributions. Ted Brandon produced a discussion paper on 'Socialism – Where do we go from here?' – for the February 1991 lunch which provoked a number of written contributions to our newsletter, the *Polemicist*. Joe Morrison opened a later lunch on 'Recession'. Professor Fred Halliday at the May 1st 1991 lunch contributed to the debate on 'The New World Order'. Fred was critical of Marxism for its underestimation of capitalism's potential and its capacity for continued expansion. It was obvious that we had by then moved away from analysing the struggles, mistakes and errors of the past, though not without recognising their eternal significance for future strategies. Still, always with us is the tragedy of the Soviet Union and the realisation of what its demise has meant in terms of the deterioration of international relations.

The Polemicist – monthly newsletter of the Anjou Club.

Economics Journalist

Monty Passes joined us for the first time in 1992, and heard the contribution of our guest, Ed Balls, at the April lunch. In a short report Monty wrote:

'Certainly, Ed's account was both interesting and informative. He explained the complicated intricacies of balance of payments deficits, public borrowing requirements, the exchange rate mechanism, the necessity of productivity and investment growth, concisely and clearly.

Yet, it was the knowledge, and the enthusiasm for knowledge, of my fellow guests which impressed me. Out of their years' of experience in which so many of them had so obviously applied, not theoretically, but pragmatic economic expertise, there evolved a stimulating and illuminating exchange of views. The questions they posed were penetrating; the answers they proposed were astute: their contributions were sophisticated and practical.'

I think that gives a true flavour of the Anjou Luncheon Club people and what motivates us to keep the Club going.

Voltaire's Bastards

Reading back numbers of the *Polemicist* newsletter is a constant reminder of how relevant and highly contemporary the ideas are that we discuss. In the report I wrote on John Ralston Saul, the Canadian Author of *Voltaire's Bastards* and who joined us in June 1993, I found the following quote: 'We live in a world in which we automatically assign blame for our failures and crimes to the irrational impulse. Our sense of man as a whole being – that is our conscious memory – has been so fractured that we have neither any philosophical or practical idea of how to hold our public and corporate authorities responsible for their actions. Deprived of our stabilising humanist roots, we are horrified to discover that the perfectly natural motive resources needed to deal with our civilisation easily degenerate into basic sentiment.'

Saul, in tracing the history of reason from Voltaire to the present day, argued that we now have, as a result of the shedding of humanist and common-sense principles, so important in the original concept, a dictatorship by a new group of pragmatic elites whose characteristic is self-assurance, cynicism, rhetoric and the worship of both ambition and power.

In my report I also wrote: 'At this time, we are assailed by sleaze in and out of government (at the time Tory), when managerial and corporate greed overwhelms the senses and when our elite replaces ordinary language with corporate, political and economic jargon, and those with power are certain they know what is best for us, rarely ask for our opinions and if they do, automatically reject them.

His (Saul's) basic argument is that a civilisation devoted to structure, expertise, specialisation and answers sees the individual citizen as a serious impediment to getting on with business.'

Today with a so-called 'New' Labour government in power I ask myself, what has changed.

Re-inventing Government
Ralston Saul was followed, as guest speaker, by Graham Mather, then President of the European Policy Forum for British and Market Studies, a Thatcherite think tank.

I had met Graham at a Charter 88 meeting, where John Smith, then leader of the Labour Party, made his last and most prestigious speech, just before his untimely death. I was impressed by the contribution Graham made and at the end approached him to join us for lunch. His chosen subject was 'Reinventing Government', on proposals then very popular in the United States and which formed a major plank in the Clinton Administration's policies. The purpose of the forum at which he spoke was, in his own description: 'To provide a new forum for discussion on the public issues critical to Britain and Europe, with an emphasis on market-led solutions and decentralised government'.

Our guests at the Anjou Club have always, even in those early days, pro-

At the House of Commons in 2004 with Ed Balls MP.

pounded ideas and opinions that have created dissension and stimulated fierce disagreements, as hinted by Saul in his thank you note to me. But never has a guest created such unity in opposition among those present as did Graham Mather. Much of what he said can be seen reflected in New Labour's programme since its first overwhelming election victory in 1997. For example, and I quote: 'The isolation of opinion other than those of policymakers, scholars, the media and business organisations, including think tanks creates and perpetuates the avoidance of controversy in matters of policy... Governments should steer and not row is the core of reinventing government'.

My note indicates that his conclusion detailed the philosophy which he claimed facilitated the peoples' demands of 'more for less'. Increased efficiency, cost effectiveness and greater consumer satisfaction would be achieved by contracting out the execution of government policy (steering) to entrepreneurial units (rowing). At the same time he claimed it to be more democratic.

How far his philosophy diverged from the overwhelming sentiments of those present can best be explained by Aldous Huxley who wrote that: 'Culture is like the sum of special knowledge that accumulates in any large united family and is the common knowledge of all its members'. It was this difference in culture and attitude to history together with the varied life experiences of those around our table that guided the arguments and the ideas that flowed readily.

Mather's apriori assumptions, propounded as history to justify the theoretical contentions of reinventing government were immediately seized upon and vociferously disputed. Why not? History is important and should be our guide to the future. As Karl Marx put it: 'To leave error unrefuted is to encourage intellectual immorality'.

Graham was given a hard time, yet on reflection, and with hindsight so much of what he said a decade or so ago rings even more harshly today. However, some of those present who attacked him, later vigorously supported, and are still supporting, not dissimilar policies being implemented under New Labour.

In reply to my letter of thanks Mather wrote: 'It was marvellous to meet you at the Gay Hussar. I did want to drop you a line to say how much I enjoyed the occasion. You have a terrific formula and some lively minds gathered around the table. For someone running a think tank it is splendid, ideas tested and batteries recharged with some new ones. Thank you very much for your hospitality at a most enjoyable occasion.'

The Housing Solution

The guest at our September 1993 lunch was Anne Power, a delightful yet tough woman. She was then Reader in Social Administration and Director of the Post-

Graduate MSc and Diploma course in the Housing Department at the London School of Economics. I wrote to Anne, after reading an article in a national newspaper on her work with Priority Estates Management about the changes made on the Hornsey Lane Estate in Crouch End, North London.

As a past secretary of a large council estate in Stamford Hill, I was particularly intrigued by this statement she made: 'Having political landlords doesn't work. People living in poor communities on no-go estates have been pushed closer and closer to the edge of society. If we can't find a way of bringing them back in − through self-management − there will be a terrible cost to society.' I could only but agree, and time has proved her words wholeheartedly prophetic.

Housing has always been an emotive and potentially manipulative issue. Political parties have in the past seen and used municipal housing as an ideological battleground. The leap-frogging promises by the main political parties as to how many homes they would build was a phenomenon of the 1960s, and was a major influence on people's voting intentions.

The policies pursued for more than a decade by Tory governments from Thatcher onwards changed the emphasis. The sales of councils' better housing properties, coupled with restrictions forbidding local authorities spending the billions of pounds received from sales, left these same councils with huge housing deficits. There is, and always has been, a link between employment and housing and these issues have always been major causes of racial friction in areas of poverty. There has always been a shameful manipulation of the housing shortage by local politicians and political parties for their own ends.

What is the way forward? Raymond Unwin, a socialist president of RIBA, some 70 years ago argued that: 'Good dwellings are part of the national wealth. They are no less so when built by a local authority, with money borrowed from its citizens than when built by a speculative house builder with money borrowed from a building society.' Anne Power argued for citizen involvement. 'Widening democracy must be more than a citizens' charter,' she said, 'we should be thinking of citizen participation and even control.'

This is exactly what she and her team, consisting mainly of volunteer residents on the Hornsey Lane Estate, wanted. They were tired of the council's dilatory responses to the never ending and constantly escalating problems they faced. Druggies, violence, disrespect and burglaries were just some of the more visible consequences of these failed policies. To quote Solly Kaye, the former East London Communist councillor who was heavily involved in housing and corruption in the sixties to eighties, in his report on Anne Power's paper: 'How welcome was the talk by Anne Power. Fired by her experiences in Britain and overseas, she is one of the pioneers charting the way to solve what to many local councils has

194

been insoluble — how to lift these housing estates, many of them vast, involving thousands, from hopelessness to hope and confidence...' Her view is that the housing problem can never be solved either by government, councils or private landlords, but only by involving the people most affected by the housing problems — the tenants. Helping, training, empowering them to manage their own estates in the interests of their community. Of course starting from where we are, this requires the co-operation of the councils concerned and in a growing number of cases this has been given with remarkable, if not sensational results.'

At the time of that talk and subsequent report, Anne had been associated with the Priority Estates Project since its inception in 1979 and she became a director in 1987, when it was transformed into an independent, non-profit making company, carrying out a wide range of work for housing organisations.

The Educationalist

Ena Abrahams has been a member of the Anjou Club almost since its inception. I first knew her when I came home to Stamford Hill on my demob from the army. She was then a teacher at Egerton Road School and had, among other trying duties, the difficult task of inducting my twin nephews with a sense of discipline so that they could remain at the school. It was a tough task, but one in which she was successful, as she has been through many of the trials and tribulations that beset her through those years. Her career in education has embraced positions at all levels almost to the very top. At our lunches she has always been a calming and influential comrade. Her knowledge of matters educational and ways of expressing what she knows are admirable and widely respected.

She was the guest speaker — we always encourage our members to take a turn at speaking — at a lunch in 1993, and her subject was 'The Tory Education Revolution'. By chance and not design it took place just prior to the publication of an alternative education strategy by IPPR, the Labour think-tank, which rejected the free-market approach to education 'because it does not work for most people — it is a blunt instrument'. Involved in the production of that document (*Education: a different vision,* IPPR £7.50) were 14 professors of education.

Of the eleven people at our lunch, four, in addition to the guest, were actively involved in education. One was a mature graduate teacher with five years' experience in primary teaching and three others were governors. The importance of having this kind of grass-roots experience was evident in the discussion that followed the excellent and meticulously prepared presentation by Ena.

There has been a catastrophic shift in the approach to, and the way people are encouraged to think about, education. Despite having been unnecessarily confrontational, the government's free market ideology has, over the past five years, been seen by some as modernisation and progress. Ena attributed this to a persistent softening-up assault on our educational system by a combination of the press, business, ideologists and politicians.

Establishing a free market ideology in education required the opening up of schools to market forces and the introduction of competition between schools as the main means of determining progress. The lack of belief on the left that there can be alternative meanings to public service, accountability and efficiency, in contrast to those expounded in Tory ideology, is hindering the revitalisation of a new vision. Educational 'reforms' instituted over the last 14 years have been part of a wider attack on public service values. As in health and other services, the methodology of the cost accountant has been chosen as the way forward.

Ena ended the discussion by stating the choices we face: either a reliance on market forces with their emphasis on a narrow educational base and divisive hierarchies of schools, or a full acceptance of education as a public good – with all that that involves.

Stalwarts
Ted Brandon has been a prolific guest speaker over many years as well as taking on the responsibility of writing, producing and distributing our monthly newsletter and giving it a much more professional appearance commensurate with Ted's marketing expertise. Monty Passes another stalwart is probably among the best read persons of my acquaintance. He should be – he has been a student for decades in his later life and has a doctorate among other achievements to his credit.

Culture and Society
In December Robert McCrum, then editor in chief at publishers Faber and Faber, was our guest. We discussed 'Culture and its place in society'. Raymond Simson, in his report, informed us that Robert came to us hot-foot from a Brighton conference on the arts and broadcasting, where he found himself in splendid isolation on the platform.

At the Anjou lunch he found himself among more kindred spirits, even if these were amicably confrontational. Certainly, when Robert mentioned the word 'culture' they did not reach for their guns, however they demanded more than lexicons to define both culture and society. Robert concentrated on three main themes: sponsorship and patronage, art and culture, heritage and English language and literature.

On the first topic, he complained about the Thatcherisation of culture, with its emphasis on return for investment. He deplored the overt censorship imposed by sponsors who generally played safe and ignored the role of the artist as a troublemaker. There was, though, some dispute about the assumed purity of patrons in the past, and no unanimity about the right of the artist to expect a special place in society.

On the second, he was on even more controversial ground, but engendered a lively discussion on high and low art. He went on to discuss British and European traditions and twentieth century changes in technology and social mores and their impact on culture and the arts. The third section was less contentious, although it was interesting to hear the most politically radical among us come down on the side of tradition in language.

As always, with a limited time for our lunch sessions, more questions were raised than answered. While there was general agreement that art was not the prerogative of the left, there was much to debate about the future of the arts and culture, conditioned as they must be by television and new technology, and by comprehensive international trends. It was agreed, though, that the arts had to survive, if not flourish, in a market-orientated culture.

The Anarchist

Our Guest in May 1992 was Colin Ward. For sure, Colin was unrecognisable as the anarchist invariably depicted in the media and by cartoonists. Our members were not sure what to expect, and nor did I when I asked Colin to talk to us about being an anarchist and to relate his beliefs to our present political and economic situation.

The first impression Colin made was most startling. As John Gorman reported: 'Colin is such an amiable man. He did not look like the popular image of an anarchist. He lacked the essential accoutrements of broad brimmed hat, black cloak and smoking bomb. On the contrary, he seemed to me to be too quiet and gentle a man to challenge authority and talk of revolution.'

As I understood him, the political philosophy of anarchism holds that it is possible and desirable to live in an egalitarian society organised without hierarchy and with no element of authority.' I reflected that Colin was talking to a group of people, many of whom had devoted a considerable part of their long lives to fighting for a dictatorship of the proletariat. Nevertheless, there were areas of common ground between us.

Colin is of the same generation as most of us present. His experiences in wartime were similar, as is his almost lifetime allegiance to a political philosophy not easily understood and much maligned. He is a prolific writer and has edited anarchist magazines since 1947. His publications are on diverse subjects and he has either written, introduced or edited over 30 books, ranging from the Folio Society's publication of Isaac Walton's *Life of John Donne* to his own thoughts

An Anjou Luncheon Club meeting with guest speaker Richard Gott on my left, in June 2006.

on Utopia for the Penguin Human Space series, to *Anarchy in Action*, published by Allen and Unwin. His latest, *Cotters and Squatters*, emphasises his dedication as an environmentalist humanist. Another publication, *Allotments: their landscape and culture,* written with David Crouch, is an example of his wider interests.'

John continued, '...as a socialist, I warmed to his vision of a society based on mutuality, without economic exploitation, without coercion and a life lived in harmony with nature. I could even accept his rejection of parliamentary democracy, for, as Oscar Wilde wrote, "Right lies not in numbers, but in reason." However, I doubted, and still doubt, that a 'News from Nowhere' society will come into being as a result of spontaneous activity without political leadership.'

John's opinion reflected the general consensus at the lunch. But, I have no doubt that many envied Colin's quiet assurance that his life and his work would eventually result in the society he envisaged.

Anarchism in London sprang from the little clubs of foreign workers that used to meet in 19th century Soho. In that sense, the Gay Hussar was an appropriate venue for Colin to express his views.

I can still recall, as a youngster in the East End of London, encountering small gatherings of elderly men avidly and heatedly discussing politics. They were Bolsheviks and Bundists, Social Democrats and Nihilists, Anarchists and Trotskyists and all had trenchant viewpoints.

Bill Fishman, in his excellent book, *The Jewish Radicals (1875-1914),* writes of gatherings of Jewish workers, young and old, meeting in Epping Forest to picnic and to listen to Rudolf Rocker, an anarchist and orator of great repute. Rocker was a German Catholic who learned to speak Yiddish fluently and was the founder of the Communist-Anarchist Yiddish language paper 'Der Arbeters Freint (The Workers Friend). His son, an acclaimed painter, who documented some of these anarchist meetings, was a great admirer of his father, but died in October 2004.

Colin Ward was proud that he had spoken on the same platform with Rocker on several occasions. He spoke of another anarchist orator of some note, Murray Buchkin, who was to visit London from North America to speak the next day at St. James's Church in Piccadilly on Eco-Anarchism. A few of us were so taken by Colin's vision that we decided to be there. John Gorman, Morry Rose, Sidney Silver and I made our way there to find the massive hall packed to the gunnels with a varied collection of almost entirely young people, probably more than a thousand. It was an exhilarating occasion, and an example of old-time oratory at its best. Good old fashioned rabble-rousing, and the response reflected that. At the end I spoke to some youngsters seated directly in front of us, whose responses attracted my attention. I asked one young girl in her late teens, whether she had enjoyed it. She replied, 'I sure did, but my mother would have enjoyed it even more'. Yes it was that old-time religion. I was reminded of the name of a left wing book I had read, called, *An Endless Adventure, an endless passion, an endless banquet* edited by Iwona Blazwick. Politics can sometimes seem that way.

A New Imperialism

Those who attended the luncheon on the 1st of April 1992 were indeed the victims of an April fool's jape. The ecstasy came first, the pain later. The polls had shown a seven point lead for Labour in the national elections as we met, and it seemed to be 'in the bag'. The discussion that day concentrated on how the next government would govern and since it was to be a Labour government, what particular problems such a 'radical' government would encounter. A lot of ground was covered. Ed Balls, the guest that day, belied his youthful appearance and dealt more than adequately with the manifest problems he himself raised and the arguments and ideas that followed.

We may have differed on many issues, but it was generally agreed that the aims and objectives would be vastly different with a Labour government in power. In the event it did not happen; once again Labour was defeated.

My own concern, expressed at the time, and at earlier lunches too, was whether Labour could achieve even the very limited programme it had put forward, and most importantly, would we ever see in Britain, or elsewhere, a Labour government willing to, or be permitted to, implement a programme with the kind of values that we have argued and fought for and that we still hold today.

There are several examples in the past of pressures being exerted on Western and, it goes without saying, third world governments, to make them conform to financial strictures and dogmas. set by outside forces. Dennis Healey, the then Labour Chancellor, was forced to turn to the International Monetary Fund to escape from an engineered Sterling crisis, and the French Socialist Party, was frustrated in applying normal Keynesian remedies when it came to power, by a run on the Franc organised by international finance.

So it was with great interest that I read an article at the end of April in the *Financial Times* by James Morgan, an economics correspondence with the BBC World Service, on that very subject. It was called 'The New Imperialism'. He responded affirmatively to my invitation and was our June guest.

Ted Brandon wrote the report. He thought, 'that James Morgan's opening remarks were extremely provocative, inferring that the world situation, in 'imperialist' terms, was, in 1992, not dissimilar to that which existed in 1912, just before the First World War. He cited the current situation in Yugoslavia, with the 'Balkanisation' of that country into individual statelets with almost the same ethnic and national make-ups that existed at the beginning of the 20th century, as an example of a move to a new imperialism. He agreed however that that interpretation was rather simplistic.

The new imperialism was infinitely more subtle than that of earlier decades. The imperialism of the latter part of the 19th century and the earlier decades of the 20th expressed itself in outright occupation and control of the colonies both politically and economically. Where the social structure was left intact, it was with the objective of a more robust control of the colonies through the intermediary role of a local middle class. In the long run the threat of armed intervention was sufficient to ensure the continued domination and the flow of profits from the colonies to the 'Mother Country'.

Morgan said that the new imperialism operated less by the threat of armed might, but rather through financial bondage, imposed by such international organisations as the International Monetary Fund, The World Bank, GATT etc. Whereas profits in the earlier era of imperialism were a direct result of material pillage of raw materials and the use of cheap local labour to undercut even home production in the pursuit of greater profits, the new imperialism culled its profits from the exorbitant interest extracted from the loans and 'aid' imposed upon developing countries.

This new imperialism was not purely concerned with economic issues in themselves, cultural and political hegemony was also part of the objective. The emphasis on a pluralistic democracy, and a free market economy was, and is, the basis on which both aid and loans are granted. It was pointed out by many that the drive for profits even in the recent past has not inhibited loans to such 'democracies' as Pinochet's Chile, Saddam's Iraq or Musharaf's Pakistan.

Political discussions at the Anjou Luncheon Club have now been going strong for more than 16 years and, we hope, will continue to do so for some time yet.

Over that period we have had over 100 guest speakers (see pages...) on the widest range of topics. Even if our deliberations will not change the world, they have been instrumental in keeping our minds active and engaged with the political and cultural processes of our times. Ideas and thoughts have no borders and can be contagious; we hope this is true of our ideas too and that comrades, friends, acquaintances and relatives — particularly our children and grandchildren — will not remain unaffected by them.

CHAPTER TWENTY SIX
And Finally...

I've often been asked how I could remain a socialist after becoming a successful businessman, rising from a poor working class background, with little formal education, to become very comfortably off. On the surface, my life story seems to offer the perfect example of what capitalism can offer everyone, i.e. the chance to get on and become rich.

I suppose it is experience rather than background that is the key. My family and relatives were generally not politically left in any way. My early experiences were undoubtedly seminal, and my reading deepened these. I held my beliefs adamantly and seriously. I was no Marxist intellectual, and would not find it easy to quote Marxist texts, but I found that instinctively, wherever I was, in whatever situations, I seemed to arrive at what I felt to be correct conclusions.

On reflection, Marxist ideas have always played a key role in my thinking. Then there was the war experience − fighting fascism − and my later involvement and dealings with the upper echelons of business people, which only served to compound my belief that there had to be a better way of running business and society in general. Nepotism, ossified class structures, blatant inefficiency, lack of foresight, indolence and ineptitude all helped confirm me in my thinking.

My own personal success and good fortune ran parallel with the failures of many hundreds of others who were trying to make a go of things as I was. I enjoyed a great deal of luck too, in particular during that period. The choices I made proved to be the correct ones.

My 80th birthday party in May 1999, attended by 220 guests, of whom over half were Morris family members.

I have no illusions that capitalism as I experienced it is the most efficient system, nor that it best serves the interests of the mass of the people. However, neither did my experiences in the Soviet Union convince me that that was the way it should or could be. So my belief in Socialism, or something akin to it, is really the baggage I've accumulated through my life, in search of the best, or as the Guardian's economics editor, Larry Elliot, puts it: 'my fantasy island'. In later years, in my never ending search for realistic solutions, I've also looked fairly deeply into the philosophies of anarchism and pacifism and, fleetingly, other fringe beliefs. While I can see some virtues in capitalism, nevertheless, despite its various transformations, it still uses the methods and clings to an ideology I abhor. Whether I am still today the socialist I was at 18, is impossible to say. But, certainly the events over this last decade and in particular the catastrophic innovations of the Blair government have convinced me that managerial elitism in the guise of New Labour is not the new and certain solution to, nor the salvation of, the capitalist ethic.

Someone who has influenced me very much over these past years, however, is the Canadian philosopher and economist, John Ralston Saul. In The Doubter's Companion he describes capitalism as: 'A concept which has moved

beyond the stage of sensible discussion. Capitalism can be a social tool or a weapon of unabashed human exploitation. Which it will be depends entirely on the way it is regulated. Capitalism itself contains no ethical values. Those who use it decide by their actions whether it is a force for good or evil... Capitalism is happiest in a non-democratic system.'

The systemic action of New Labour is without ideology or a semblance of socialist ideas. It has exorcised controlling regulations, neutered trade unionism and attacked democratic institutions whenever deemed necessary in its attempt to be a major player in the world of globalisation. Its disastrous adventure in Iraq has created a smouldering furnace which inevitably will have a catastrophic affect in the immediate future. To my mind New Labour has been a force for evil.

These memories I have written here are not definitive. My life in travel continues to this very day. In retail sales with Travex Tours, operating one of the first legal 'bucket shops' through Vantage Holidays, and forming Chancery Cruises as a pioneering theme cruise company, while at the same time being involved with ABTA and acting as chair and founder of the Travel Agents Study Group. But my political life has never subsided. Through all these years I have participated in whichever way I could at any particular time, and this will continue.

Above all else I recognize that the most treasured memories are of those who have freely given me their love and affection something I have always cherished and for which I shall continue to be grateful. The guidance and support of so many has been invaluable; maybe just a single word or small gesture has touched me sufficiently to make a difference. I sincerely hope that I have been a similar inspiration to the many whose lives have crossed mine in whatever sphere or period of my life.

ANJOU CLUB SPEAKERS

ABRAHAMS	Ena	HALLIDAY	Fred	PERRYMAN	Mark
AITKENHEAD	Decca	HEWITT	Patricia	PALAST	Greg
ALLEN	Mike	HOSTETTLER	John	POTTINS	Charles
BALLS	Ed	HODKINSON	Stuart	POWELL	Annie
BARNETT	Anthony	HUTCHINSON	Gordon	POWER	Mike
BARD	Julia	HUTTON	Will	QUINN	Michael
BAXTER	Sarah	JACQUES	Martin	REY	Joshua
BECKETT	Francis	JACOBS	Stephen	RIVLIN	Michael
BENN	Tony	JOHNSTONE	Monty	ROTBLATT	Joseph
BENTON	Sarah	JONES	Lynne	ROSE	John
BRANDON	Edward	KATZ	Phil	ROSEN	Harold
BRINDLE	David	KAUFMAN	Chris	RODIN	Jeff
BRETMAN	Ian	KAYE	Solly	RUSSELL	Earl
BUNTING	Madeleine	KEEGAN	William	SAUL	John R
CAULKIN	Simon	KINGSNORTH	Paul	SAVILLE	John
CLOAKE	Martin	KINSMAN	Francis	SASSOON	Donald
COATES	Ken	KOSSOFF	Gideon	SCOTT	Stafford
COATES	Barry	LEE	Michael	SEDDON	Mark
COHEN	Nick	LEFTON	Charles	SIVANANDAN	Ambalavaner
COLLINS	Tish	LEYS	Colin	SHINER	Phil
COOPER	Yvette	LLOYD	John	SHINDLER	Colin
CORBYN	Jeremy	MATHER	Graham	SHISHKOVSKY	Seyavan
CURTIS	Mark	METH	Monty	SILVER	Sidney
CONWAY	David	MORGAN	James	SIMON	Roger
DURDEN-SMITH	Jo	MORTIMER	Jim	TEMPLE	Nina
ELLIOTT	Larry	MORRISON	Joe	TIMMS	Dave
ELWORTHY	Scilla	MORRIS	Aubrey	TODD	Ron
FISHER	Mark	MORRIS	Lawrence	TRIESMAN	David
FREEDLAND	Jonathon	MOSS	Bernie	WARD	Colin
GABLE	Gerry	MONKS	Pieta	WAINWRIGHT	Hilary
GOLDBERG	Dennis	McCRUM	Robert	WALKER	David
GOODMAN	Geoffrey	McIVOR	Martin	WATERS	Steve
GOTT	Richard	NEWENS	Stan	WEIGHTMAN	Gavin
GREEN	Duncan	NOVAK	Kalo	WILLMORE	Ian
GROSZ	Stephen	PANITCH	Leo	YOUNGE	Gary
GUNWELL	Barbara	PASSES	Monty	ZANGANA	Haifa